Ashley Blake

Shining Bright Lights
In Dark Places

Finders Publishing

First published in Great Britain by Finders Publishing

© Ashley Blake 2011

Finders
Kemp House
152-160 City Road
London EC1V 2NX

ISBN 978-0-9570004-0-7

Typeset in Palatino Linotype

To My Mother,
Jess,
Abi, Cheryl, Diane
and Calam

'Friendship is when people know all about you but like you anyway': a quote from an unknown author.

Throughout my short but varied life I've been fortunate enough to have met many wonderful people. Some, I've been lucky to have shared an intimate relationship with, others have been really good friends.

Journeying along life's twisty path inevitably means even the closest of friendships are tested from time to time and it is only then that we're reminded how lucky and how loved we are.

I'm guilty of taking many things for granted, my health, my family, my friends, my freedom but no longer. It's only when they're taken from us do we realize just what we had.

I cannot begin to thank all the people who supported me through the dark days, your unconditional love did more than help get me through.

Therefore, I would like to dedicate this book to my three sisters Abi, Cheryl and Diane, who have always protected their little brother. To our Mum who's no longer with us, a strong, loving and simply gorgeous woman who deserved a better life. To my friends who've stood by me and assured me that it'll all turn out okay in the end, and for allowing me the privilege of *being your mate*. To my son Calam whose love I will always appreciate and never take for granted again.

Also to Jessica Katie Hayes, with whom I had the utmost privilege to spend eight years of my life. As you read on you'll discover that Jess also served my prison sentence, but on the outside. Jess had every opportunity to leave but she stood by her man throughout. Had it not been for this remarkable woman things would have been very different, I need say no more.

Jessica and I lived the dream, it's a great shame that it ended with a nightmare. Jess, I will always love you

Introduction

So, there I was enjoying a great TV career, a not so successful restaurant business. I had a wonderful girlfriend who I was sure to marry. I had a great group of friends who'd die for me, and I for them. Then it all changed in a second, everything, gone. You're about to read how life can turn on a sixpence just when you least expect it and when it does, it's a great leveler. You really know who's with you and who's against you. How I fell from being a bright star on BBC television into the darkness of a prison cell. At the time I kept a diary of the nightmare I was faced with as a way of trying to make sense of what was happening to me and, of course, as a journalist my instinct compelled me to write. Either way this is a true account of what happened whilst I was banged up in one of the country's most notorious jails. I haven't changed the names to protect the guilty.

The Place 2B

I was flying high in a great television career, a reporter on BBC Watchdog, traveling the world for the BBC's *Holiday* programme, the presenter of the successful weekly current affairs, *Inside Out*, and BBC regional news, *Midlands Today*. Turn on your TV and there was every chance you'd see me on primetime television every day. Life was good, I had just met a fabulous woman who had the personality to deal with my high profile, I had a wonderful family and a great network of true friends who'd known me for decades and whose main responsibility was to keep my feet firmly on the ground should I show any signs of becoming a diva.

I'd been on the telly for quite a number of years and I was lucky to have achieved most of what I wanted from my career so far. It was for this reason that I decided to diversify my talents and have a go at running my own business.

My local bar, which I'd used as a regular with my friends for the last ten years, was struggling to keep afloat. My girlfriend Jess was at the top of her career as the Public Relations Manager for the *Spearmint Rhino* Gentlemen's group of clubs and wanted a change. It was the perfect solution, fate had brought us together to run our own business, a dream many share but few realize. We had the money, we had a certain amount of experience, and we had great ideas to turn the large old pub into a successful restaurant. So, between us, we bought it and moved in, that was December 2003.

We both totally underestimated how much hard work it is to run your own business, but we were dedicated to making our restaurant and bar, *The Place 2B*, live up to the name we'd chosen. We were rewarded for our hard work during the first few years with a healthy balance sheet and some great loyal customers. I had kept my job at the BBC, but would start every day at the business which was also our home. I would spend the dawn hours of each morning sorting anything the business required from fixing leaking pipes, broken toilets, gardening, changing light bulbs, to checking deliveries, before donning my suit and tie, and heading off to present the day's news on the BBC. Jess would run our business on a day to day basis, employing staff, greeting customers, negotiating prices with suppliers, paying bills and so on.

It wasn't until smoking in public places was banned in England on 1st July 2007 that we began to feel the effects of a downturn in trade. That, coupled with the onset of a recession meant that it wasn't long before *The Place 2B* began to struggle. Despite being the only Thai restaurant in an affluent area of Birmingham, with an excellent reputation for quality food and great atmosphere, it seemed impossible to get people out of their homes as their purse too was being squeezed by the poor economy. However, all was not lost, I still had a very good day job at the BBC which funded any shortfall our business suffered. Not the ideal solution, but it would allow us to continue in the hope that the recession would pass by. Besides, I had the responsibility of a small staff to pay whose livelihood depended on us.

We had a dedicated staff who worked extremely hard to help us keep our nose above water. We dropped prices, we marketed ourselves as a celebratory venue, and became *The Place 2B* for weddings, birthday parties, christenings, funerals, comedy nights, anything we could think of to get customers in. Eighteen hour days became the norm, extremely hard work for little or even no reward.

One of our team was a young girl called Rachel who had joined us as a waitress aged just sixteen. She was very good at her job, and was popular with the staff and customers. Rachel was a hard worker and on numerous occasions would happily agree to work at the last minute when another member of staff had let us down.

In January 2009 she was about to turn eighteen years of age. Rachel was planning to mark her coming of age with a party and asked Jess and I whether we would host it at the restaurant. At first we reacted with a definite *no*. Our experience suggested that 18th birthday parties are trouble, simply because young people and alcohol do not make a good mix. It was for this reason that we had never hosted an 18th birthday party at *The Place 2B* during the six years we'd owned it. Rachel was clearly disappointed judging by the expression on her face. Later that evening I spoke to Jess. I told her I was upset that we were unable to host the birthday celebrations, and continued by reflecting on how Rachel had helped us to grow the business, reminding us both of the number of times she had helped us out with staffing problems. Jess agreed, and she began to feel equally as bad as I did. Thus we came to the conclusion that we should host Rachel's eighteenth, but there were to be specific conditions attached:

1. There was to be no underage drinking
2. The party would end no later than 2.00am
3. Her parents had to attend.

Three simple conditions which Rachel was happy to adhere to, and so it went ahead.

Saturday 24th January 2009.

Rachel, Jess and I began to set out the party, including decorating the restaurant with balloons, party poppers, posters and millions upon millions of those annoying little glittering, '18' sprinkly things scattered everywhere. Come 7.30pm the place looked every bit 'party central'. The guests began arriving shortly after 7.30pm, including several sets of parents, my staff had been briefed by Jess to I.D. anyone they suspected of being under the age to buy alcohol.

By 9.00pm Rachel's party was in full swing, the party girl absolutely the center of attention, just the way it should be. More and more of her friends arrived by the minute, the atmosphere was brilliant.

By 12 midnight the party was the success we planned it to be, the music was pumping, people were bouncing, the tills were kerrchinging, and everyone was having a fabulous time.

At 12.30am Jess complained of having a headache and told me she was going to leave to stay at her sister's house, because of the noise there was no way she would get any peace if she retired to our upstairs home. She confirmed

"I'll be okay", to which I assured her I would be too, as everyone was having such a good time and there was only one and a half hours to go before the end of the party.

By this time the small group of parents had chosen to leave.

At the stroke of 2.00am the DJ brought his last song to a close, and the lights went up on cue. The crowd of young revellers was disappointed that their night of enjoyment was over, and drunkenly chanted for one more song to be played. To my staff and I this was a familiar sign that all had enjoyed themselves and the night was a success, but my first rule of a good night at *The Place 2B* was; always leave them wanting more.

With the restaurant now in full illumination, Rachel's sixty or so guests began to leave. The staff and I began the task of clearing up. It didn't take long for the building to empty as everyone made their way to the car park and the awaiting taxis.

Just then I was called to a commotion happening outside. As I walked through the main doors onto the car park I could see an off duty member of my staff arguing with four or five lads. It was a simple disagreement, so I intervened by taking my staff member away from the confrontation and back into the bar to prevent the problem from escalating. As I turned away I glimpsed a further clash happening to my left. Before I could work out what was going on I noticed a lad on the floor surrounded by a group of around fifteen young men and women. As I went over to see whether I could help, the group set upon yet another lad who I knew as Steve, a regular customer of mine. I was confused as to what was going on, and I asked everyone to calm down so we could find out what had happened, however, they were determined to continue their attack on him. A succession of blows from the angry group of drunken young men knocked Steve to the floor, and he appeared to be dazed. I called for Matt, my bar manager to call the police, he came out and dragged Steve by the arms back inside the building and shut the doors. The small group of people began to swell as they became more and more angry, demanding that Steve should come back out. I was joined by my one and only doorman on duty that night, Mario. We both stood in the doorway to the building trying to work out what was going on. The crowd of angry young men and women were hard to understand, but they made their intention very clear. They wanted to go back inside the restaurant to fetch Steve. When we wouldn't allow them access they turned their aggression on us. As they began pushing forward, we were being slapped, punched, and kicked by young lads and young girls. They were swearing and shouting racial abuse at Mario and me, calling him a 'polish bastard', (he's from Albania), and me, 'black bastard nigger'. I heard jeers of 'get the news reader'.

As the crowd pushed Mario and I back towards the doors, kicking and punching, I believed the police would arrive at any moment, we had to just stop them from getting back into the restaurant, but there was no sign of any help.

Built in 1939, the building is over seventy years old, the main doors are original, and subsequently very flimsy, and insecure. When the restaurant is closed they are wedged shut with a pole to make them secure. I thought about getting inside and waiting for the police to arrive, but if I allowed the crowd anywhere near the doors it wouldn't take long to break through. As the crowd advanced they became more and more aggressive, bottles and ash trays from the smoking area began to rain down on us. The aluminum tables and chairs were being broken up and thrown at us, there were missiles coming from all areas. Mario grabbed a table to use as a shield, my bar manager Matt appeared in the doorway. I rushed past him into the restaurant to retrieve the pole. My thought was to get Mario behind the doors, wedge them shut and wait for the police.

As I returned to the doorway, Mario was surrounded by the crowd, he was being kicked and punched from all sides. I grabbed at his belt to pull him into the doorway but the crowd turned on me. I lifted the pole above my head and shouted

"Get back, get back."

This threat seemed to work as much of the crowd moved away, but it was only for a few seconds. My threat had angered a small group of lads to my right who felt brave enough to advance towards us again. They were joined by others. I was determined, more so this time, not to let the crowd anywhere near me as they were holding bits of broken garden furniture and broken bottles in their hands, they were baying for blood. I held the pole up, swinging it above my head and out towards the crowd, shouting "get back, get back" and praying for the police to arrive soon.

This was the point at which I felt most scared. I truly feared for my life as the thirty-strong crowd all seemed hell bent on attacking me. Where were the police? I couldn't even hear any sirens. "If any of those people get near me I'm going to die", I thought. It was like a riot, I saw my business being broken up and couldn't understand why. It had been a great night, I wondered why this crowd was smashing up our business? A business we'd worked so hard at for years to make a success. They didn't care a jot, they were angry, very angry, their anger was fueled by alcohol, their tempers giving them the strength to rip apart my garden furniture with their bare hands to use as missiles and weapons to hit me with. Why weren't they running away? There was nothing stopping them. I didn't chase after anyone, I just stood my ground waving the pole and shouting for them to get back. I was defending myself, my business, my home, my staff, and the customer who'd started the whole thing.

After what seemed like an eternity a single police car arrived, but the officer inside chose to stay put until others arrived. He must have witnessed what looked like a riot. To my relief it wasn't long before more cars arrived and the place was swarming with coppers.

Inside the restaurant I was surrounded by frightened, hysterical staff who I tried to comfort. A police inspector introduced himself and began to try to work out what had happened. Although I was confused about it all, I gave him all the details I could. He asked to see any CCTV footage and, along with a young male officer, I invited him upstairs to my living quarters where we kept the recording equipment.

As the officers shuffled through the footage, I left in search of cigarettes to calm my nerves. I went back down to the restaurant to check that everyone was okay. While I was there it was suggested by a member of staff that I get rid of the pole I had been swinging as it could look bad. I went behind the bar to the back of the fridge, took the pole, and threw it out through the back doors into the garden. I returned to the police upstairs who told me that they were seizing the recording equipment to be used as evidence, naturally I agreed. The officers stopped talking momentarily as they each listened to their radios via earpieces. Once their communication had finished they informed me that they were arresting me on suspicion of assault, causing injury to a seventeen year old man. It was the first I knew of such a thing.

As I left the restaurant I was escorted to my car where I was allowed to retrieve a coat. When the two officers and I made our way across the car park a small group of youths were still milling about. They caught sight of me and began to shout

"There he is, that's the black bastard."

I complained to the officers about racial abuse who responded by telling the youths to go away. I got my coat and was taken to the police station.

As I was interviewed I was still in shock, I was bewildered and scared. I began to tell the police my version of events as best as I could remember. It was put to me that I deliberately attacked a young man with a pole causing him facial injuries, and that several witnesses had confirmed this. Of course I denied I had attacked anyone, or caused any injuries.

"That's a lie" I was told by the officers.

Again and again they accused me of deliberately arming myself, and intentionally attacking a young man. It all began to look bad, very bad. Between interviews I desperately tried to work out what had happened and why I was the one in this situation. I was tired and unable to think straight. As the adrenalin subsided I could feel the pain in my face and head having received several blows from the crowd. My thoughts turned to my job, "this is surely going to be in the papers, I'll lose my job, a career I have spent years working hard at, my livelihood, my reputation, all in tatters, why are they doing this to me?"

In the second and third interview, with advice from my solicitor, I told the police that I was acting in self-defence, and maintained that I did not deliberately arm myself, or hit anyone with a pole. They showed me the CCTV footage seized from my business which clearly showed me entering the bar area and picking up the pole from behind the fridge then going back through the doors. To them this was evidence that I had armed myself. I explained that I retrieved the pole in order to secure the front doors to prevent the crowd from entering the restaurant. However, when I went back to get Mario, he was surrounded by the crowd and being attacked so I used the pole to threaten them by swinging it above my head. The officers asked whether I had deliberately targeted anyone and struck them in the face, to which I answered

"No I did not". The officer continued,

"Do you accept that while you were swinging the pole above your head you could have made contact with someone"?

I answered "Well, I guess it was possible, but I don't remember making contact with anyone. If anyone was injured it was not as a result of me hitting them, they must have got the injuries from somewhere else, there were a lot of missiles being thrown".

(We don't have CCTV cameras on the outside of the building so it was impossible for me to prove what was going on as I went back through the front doors.)

I was shown a photograph. It was of a young man's lower face. The left side of his bottom lip was cut and looked disgusting. I was told that I had deliberately caused the injury, and that the young man needed ten stitches and would be scarred for life. I denied I had anything to do with the wound, and suggested that he must have been caught in the cross fire and hit by a missile thrown by the crowd of which he was a part, but they refused to believe me and I was charged!

To this day Rachel, our young waitress, the birthday girl, still believes it was all her fault. Rachel, it was not.

The following headlines appeared in the local and national press.

BBC presenter hit teenager in face with wooden pole, court told

CHRISTINA SAVVAS
Staff Reporter

Midland TV presenter Ashley Blake hit a teenager with a wooden pole during a violent disturbance outside his bar, a court has heard.

The 40-year old BBC newsreader swung the patio umbrella pole above his head and struck 17-year-old Greg Jones in the face after an 18th birthday party being held at The Place 2 B in Sutton Coldfield on Chester Road.

He appeared before Birmingham Crown Court and denied wounding with intent to cause grievous bodily harm and unlawful wounding.

Birmingham-born Blake who ran the venue with his partner Jessica Hayes but has since left, also pleaded not guilty to attempting to perverting the course of justice by throwing the pole into a neighbouring garden centre in an attempt to conceal it from police after the incident in the early hours of January 25.

The prosecution told the jury that Blake ran into the bar to fetch the three-foot pole after 17-year-old Adam Finn was punched and left unconscious. Steven Sproule, 38, of Booths Farm Road, Great Barr, Birmingham, has pleaded guilty to assault occasioning actual bodily harm.

The prosecution said Mr Jones was attempting to calm the group down when they became angry and upset.

Naomi Gilchrist, prose-

Ashley Blake arrives for court

cuting, said: "The defendant was stood in front of the group. Greg Jones asked him to call an ambulance and heard no response.

"He noticed the defendant had a pole in his hands as if to threaten him with it. The defendant swung the pole above his head and hit Greg Jones in the face with it. Mr Jones stumbled back and put his hand to his face when he noticed a lot of blood. He had blood all over his hands, his face and clothing."

Miss Gilchrist added: "The pole, after it was used by the defendant to hit Greg Jones, was put back behind the bar by the bar manager but the pole did not remain behind the bar.

"Shortly after police arrived on the scene, the defendant took it and he disposed of it by throwing it over the fence into the garden centre next door."

The court heard that Blake told police officers at the scene that he needed to go to the toilet – but went to get rid of the pole instead.

He was then arrested after witnesses said he was responsible for the attack.

During the police first interview, Blake denied getting the pole. When shown CCTV footage fetching it from the bar, he said he was going to use it to secure the doors and protect his staff from the revellers who were throwing objects. He denies hitting anyone with the pole.

Blake has not appeared on screen since being charged.

The trial continues.

TV star 'attacked teen with a pole'

By Christina Savvas

BBC newsreader Ashley Blake attacked a teenager with a wooden pole after a party at his former Birmingham bar, a court heard.

The 40-year-old Midlands Today presenter allegedly swung the patio umbrella pole above his head and struck 17-year-old Greg Jones in the face following an 18th birthday bash at The Place 2B in Chester Road, New Oscott, in the early hours of January 25.

Blake has denied wounding with intent to cause grievous bodily harm and unlawful wounding. He has also pleaded not guilty to attempting to pervert the course of justice by throwing the pole into a neighbouring garden centre in an attempt to conceal it from police.

Naomi Gilchrist, prosecuting, told the jury at Birmingham Crown Court that Blake ran into the bar to fetch the pole – three feet long and one-and-a-half inches wide with a screw sticking out of it – after 17-year-old Adam Finn was punched and left unconscious by customer Steven Sproule.

The jury was told that Sproule, 38, of Booths Farm Road, Great Barr, had pleaded guilty to assault occasioning actual bodily harm.

"Greg Jones asked the defendant to call an ambulance and heard no response," Ms Gilchrist said.

"He noticed the defendant threaten him with it. The defendant swung the pole above his head and hit Greg Jones in the face with it.

"Mr Jones stumbled back and put his hand to his face when he noticed a lot of blood. He had blood all over his hands, his face and clothing."

Ms Gilchrist added: "The pole, after it was used by the defendant to hit Greg Jones, was put back behind the bar by the bar manager but the pole did not remain behind the bar.

"Shortly after police arrived on the scene the defendant took it and he disposed of it by throwing it over the fence into the garden centre next door."

During the first interview with police, Blake denied getting the pole.

When shown CCTV footage of him fetching it from the bar, he said he was going to use it to secure the doors and protect his staff from the revellers who had begun throwing items of furniture. He denies hitting anyone with the pole.

Blake, who no longer runs the venue, has not appeared on screen since being charged.

He worked as the BBC's regional art and entertainment correspondent and worked as a presenter on consumer programme Watchdog before moving back to Birmingham, where he could be seen regularly presenting Midlands Today and Inside Out.

BBC news star denies attack

FULL STORY: PAGE 5

I was taken off screen with immediate effect at the BBC and given a desk job. My bosses were careful neither to be seen to be supporting me, nor dropping me like a hot stone. I'd been a hard-working, loyal member of the team for almost ten years

27

and I had a blemish free record, I hadn't even had so much as a day off sick in all that time, but the BBC had to be seen to be doing the right thing. My colleagues were all extremely supportive and concerned, and being some of the finest journalists in the country they all wanted to know the details of what happened.

My first Crown Court appearance didn't happen until 27th April 2009. It was a miserable, dull, drizzly Monday morning when I was woken by the alarm clock at 7.30am. Within seconds of switching on my mobile phone it began to beep with messages of support from friends and family. I even received a text message from the mother of a little boy called Dylan, on whom I'd reported a story some time ago. It read:

Hi Ashley.
Good luck today,
I hope all goes well.
Hope to see you back on the telly soon, love n best wishes
Dawn, Dylan and family xxx.

It was sent at 7.41am. No sooner had I read that than the phone beeped again. This time it was a message from Rachel, the series director on my programme *Inside Out*, it read:

Be strong. You're surrounded by love x.

Another from a West Midlands Police firearms officer, a friend of many years:

All the very best for today,
we'll keep our fingers X'ed for you.

The messages kept coming, at times preventing me from getting ready to be at court on time.

Jess and I arrived at the court at 9.30am on the dot. We were met by a photographer who I recognized from working at various events or stories I'd been sent to report on over the years.

"I hate to have to ask Ash, but can I get a picture?" I agreed, he snapped away, shook my hand and wished me the best of luck.

The case was being heard in Court No.17. Just outside were around twenty people, police officers, reporters, including a colleague, court staff, barristers, and eight young, scruffy looking lads wearing jeans, trainers and sports tops. I didn't recognize any of them and wondered if they were part of the group that attacked me that night. I was taken inside where a female security officer unlocked the door to the thick, bullet-proof, glass fronted dock. I was joined by Steve, my co-defendant, and the process began.

The charges were read out to me and I was asked to enter my plea.

Wounding with intent?
"Not guilty."

Conspiracy to pervert the course of justice?
"Not guilty."

Affray?
"Not guilty."

There were more discussions between the silks, and a trial date was set for Monday 27th July 2009, my first appearance was over and I was free to go, for the time being at least.

The gravitas of the situation I was in took its toll. I was the subject of speculation, criticism, and at times ridicule. Depression, sleepless nights, stressful days followed. I had the support of close friends, wonderful colleagues, much of the viewing public, but not least my truly wonderful girlfriend and soul mate Jess. Together we battled on.

Monday 27th July 2009. The Trial

I won't go into all the detail of the trial as that would just take too long but, like with all court trials, they're made up of two sides who battle it out using facts and the power of persuasion to convince a jury who's right and who's wrong. I will say though that all involved did agree, in general, on the sequence of events of the night of the 24th January. However, the charges against me had changed. I was now charged with the very serious offence of Section 18; Assault, Causing Grievous Bodily Harm With Intent, the less serious offence of Section 20; Assault, Causing Grievous Bodily Harm Without Intent, and Conspiracy to Pervert The Course of Justice for throwing the pole into the garden. At the end of the five day trial the jury was sent out to consider its verdict. The jury came back.

"To the charge of Section 18, Assault, Causing Grievous Bodily Harm with Intent, how do you find the defendant, guilty or not guilty?"

"NOT GUILTY."

There were cheers from the public gallery, I remained motionless, there was more to come.

"On the count of Section 20 Assault, Causing Grievous Bodily Harm *without* Intent, do you find the defendant guilty or not guilty?"

"GUILTY!"

The public gallery fell silent, I almost fainted. Being found guilty of this charge meant I was automatically found guilty of *Conspiring to Pervert the Course of Justice.*

The verdict was repeated to me by the judge but none of it was sinking in, I was in total shock. Despite being found guilty the judge deferred sentencing, and ordered that I return to the court on the 2nd September 2009. He told me it was inevitable that I faced a custodial sentence, but before deciding how long he would read pre-sentence reports prepared by the probation service. I was released from the dock in a daze. Jess and I couldn't believe what was happening. Outside the court a press pack had gathered, snappers, TV news crews, reporters. These were my friends, my colleagues, and they too were shocked but needed a quote from me for the evening news programme. Usually comfortable in front of a TV camera I couldn't find any words to describe how I felt. A lifetime of hard work, my career, my business, everything had just ended.

During the next month I prepared a dossier of character references, and evidence of all the good charity work I'd been involved in over the years to try to convince the judge that, despite being found guilty by a group of my peers, I'm not a bad person, and I did not deserve a prison sentence. I wasn't short of people who would come forward to offer to write words of support to the judge:

August 17 2009

Dear Judge Carr

I am writing to tell you a little more about my good friend Ashley Blake. I have known Ashley for eight years. We first met as work colleagues at the BBC. We both joined Midlands Today at the same time and as the new boy and girl hit it off straight away.

When I first met him all I saw was a very confident and suave chap. It took a little more time to get to know the real man behind the smile and infectious sense of humour but it didn't take long to find the kind, quite serious and generous side of Ash.

He lost his mum to cancer and that has, understandably, affected him ever since. In fact every August at his former bar and restaurant, the Place 2B, he held summer balls in memory of his mother and to raise thousands for the charity that helped her, the Cancer Macmillan Nurses. Myself, my husband and many friends and work colleagues went and he made sure that we all had a super time. He put so much effort and work into those events, organising bands, entertainment and a marquee but to be honest for him it was a labour of love. He never bragged about how much he raised or how much hard work it was, he just got on with it.

From the outside his natural charm and ability made his rise to TV presenter look easy, the reality I know was far from that and he used to joke: "I'm just a rough kid from Handsworth me." What an inspiration that kid from Handsworth was to young people. Ashley never tried to cover up his background or pretend he was something he was not. In fact he visited schools and inspired young people to show them they too could have great careers and had more to look forward to than a life of crime and the dole.

It's those kind of actions that I associate with Ash, not one of violence. In fact I can say hand on heart I have never seen him argue or raise his voice. If tempers get frayed he's the peacemaker who uses comedy to diffuse the situation and it's that attitude that makes him so popular.

Throughout his recent ordeal I have kept in regular contact and despite the fact it's his life that has been turned upside down and left in ruins, he is the one when I speak to him to ask : "How are you?".

Ash is a true friend, who has had one hell of a journey to ensure he didn't make crime his life. He broke the mould to build a fabulous career. I am proud to be his friend.

Yours sincerely

Suzanne Virdee.

34

August 26th 2009

To whom it may concern,

I write in reference to Ashley Blake. I work with disabled children and I have known Ashley for many years.

He always has time for everyone and is polite, thoughtful and kind.

Over the years Ashley has raised a great deal of money for charity and has never stinted in his support for a charitable appeal.

I hope the court can bear in mind Ashley's kindness and consideration and his charity work. I think it is important that the court knows about the kind of person Ashley is, about the good work he has done and about the many people he has helped without any thought of return for himself. I would be very happy to come to court to speak on Ashley's behalf if required.

Yours,

Christine Hart,
(Registered foster carer and respite worker with disabled children)

Principal
Mr D.A. Seddon MA

Vice Principals
Mrs J.Coleman MBE MA NPQH
Ms C.Gibson MA NPQH

Major Sponsors:
3E's Alliance in Partnership; Bentways Holdings;
Kidderminster Education Trust; Kidderminster Youth Trust;
Mercers' Company, Shirelands Language College; Thomas
Telford School; Veldoon Printers Ltd; W.M. Co-op; Wilkinson

BAXTER
Business and Enterprise
COLLEGE

Habberley Road
Kidderminster
Worcestershire
DY11 5RQ

Tel: 01562 741524
Fax: 01562 827719
info@baxtercollege.worcs.sch.uk
www.baxtercollege.worcs.sch.uk

DS/ALC

13th August 2009

Judge Peter Carr
Birmingham Crown Court
4 Roman Place
Sutton Coldfield
BIRMINGHAM
B74 3FJ

Dear Sir

Re: Ashley Blake - Character Reference

It has been my privilege to know Ashley Blake for over 5 years and during that time he has always impressed me with his natural empathy for people and children, in particular. He has worked closely with me and our school and our students always appreciate his sense of fun but also his sensitivity. We are classed as a challenging school and Ashley is able to draw on his own experiences to provide the role model figure that has proved so valuable here.

Ashley Blake is a good man, community-spirited with real integrity. I can only see this recent altercation as an aberration – a one off, because it doesn't tally with the man that we know who takes his community duties so responsibly. I ask you to take this into consideration when deliberating over your verdict.

Yours sincerely

D A Seddon
Principal

36

Justice Carr

Birmingham Crown Court

2nd Floor
Delta View
Coventry Road
Sheldon
Birmingham B26 3PG
tel 0121 742 6393
fax 0121 722 2016

WE ARE MACMILLAN. CANCER SUPPORT

<u>Character Reference for Mr Ashley Blake</u>

<u>Strictly Not For Public Disclosure</u>

Mr Ashley Blake has actively supported Macmillan Cancer Support in the Midlands for a number of years. Mr Blake chose to support Macmillan as a charity following the loss of his mother to cancer in 2000 during which time the family received valuable support from the Macmillan Nurses.

The Birmingham Fundraising Team at Macmillan have worked with Mr Blake for the last few years primarily in organising Summer Balls held at his bar and restaurant The Place 2B with all funds raised being donated to Macmillan. Over the last 2 years these Summer Balls have raised nearly £2,500 for the charity and Mr Blake has been key in promoting these events locally and raising awareness for the cause. He has also supported the fundraising team on an ongoing basis with a variety of projects.

While working with Mr Blake over the last few years, we have always found him to be extremely supportive, polite and generous. He has been a great ambassador for Macmillan locally and has been willing to share his own personal story to inspire others to fundraise for us.

Over the years we have greatly appreciated the help he has provided to us locally and it has been a pleasure working with him.

Yours faithfully

Sharon Battersby
On behalf of the Birmingham & Black Country Fundraising Team

37

16 - 8 - 09

Dear Judge Carr,

I am writing to you about Ashley Bale. I have known and worked with Ashley at the BBC in Birmingham for about eight years and, during that time, he has become a trusted friend and colleague. He has been an extremely popular figure in our newsroom and a highly valued member of our broadcasting team. A number of assignments he has covered for the BBC have involved a certain amount of danger, including direct threats to him, and these have always been handled sensitively and courageously, with care, discretion and dignity.

As a friend, I find his current predicament immensely difficult to comprehend. He has no natural tendency towards conflict or aggression and it is hard to imagine him acting in a confrontational way unless he was feeling fearful and under threat.

I was surprised to learn that he had previous convictions, albeit from many years ago, but I noted that none of these incidents involved violence.

As far as my experience is concerned, Ashley is a loyal, supportive and trustworthy individual whose current plight is totally out of character.

Thank you for taking the time to read this letter,

Yours sincerely,

Nick Orson

Character Reference for Ashley Blake

Prepared by Rachel Bowering, Series Director, BBC Television.

I worked with Ashley Blake on the BBC Current Affairs Programme, Inside Out, from 2003 to 2009. As his director we worked together on location, recording his pieces to camera and I produced several films which he presented. It was always a pleasure to work with Ashley, his enthusiasm is infectious, his commitment admirable and when working with me he consistently pushed himself to deliver his best performance.

His talent as a presenter is rare. He's well planned, punctual, calm and arrived on location with an appetite for the job. If members of the public stopped us when filming, he took the time to talk to them, sign autographs or have his photograph taken, people felt included. I've only ever thought of Ashley as a true professional who showed consideration for his colleagues and the people whose story we were telling. His attitude and commitment to our work has helped make my time on Inside Out a pleasure.

Outside of work he was always willing to support local charities and schools. On many occasions after a days work with us, he was heading of to hand out prizes at a school awards evening, open a church fete or host a charity evening. I know he always tried to accommodate such requests as he did for me twice at local schools. He gave his time freely and willingly and always with a smile.

Rachel Bowering

Baby Lifeline, Empathy Enterprise Building, Bramston Crescent, Tile Hill, Coventry CV4 9SW.
Tel: 024 7642 2135 Fax: 024 7642 2136
Email: info@babylifeline.org.uk Web: www.babylifeline.org.uk

FOR THE URGENT ATTENTION OF HIS HONOUR JUDGE PETER CARR

Birmingham Crown Court

18th August 2009

Your Honour

Mr Ashley Blake – Due for Sentencing – 2nd September 2009

I understand that the above named is due to be sentenced on the above date. I would respectfully ask this Honourable Court to take into consideration the following testimonial.

Mr Blake has been an Honorary Vice President of the Baby Lifeline Charity for at least three years. He has always given of his personal time generously for the purpose of fund-raising events and media campaigns and this has proved very valuable for the Charity because of his high profile. Mr Blake has always been patient and kind in all of his dealings with the Charity and our supporters.

On a more personal note, I am shocked that Mr Blake finds himself in this situation as all evidence of his nature to date has been to the contrary. I am aware that in all probability a young and promising media career has now been blighted (at least temporarily if not permanently) and I can only hope that this Honourable Court will bear this in mind when imposing sentence.

Thank you for taking the time to read this letter.

Yours faithfully

Judy Ledger
Founder & Chief Executive

41

Date: 14 August 2009

Ref: Mr. Ashley Blake

Dear Sir

I am pleased to offer a reference for Mr. Blake, I have had the pleasure of knowing him for 5 years since he took over the tenancy of the Place 2 B, during this time I have not only come to know him as personal friend but also as a business associate.

In all my dealings with Mr. Blake I have known him to be polite and courteous individual who is always more than willing to help out others, together with his partner Jess they ran a convivial restaurant/bar with a welcoming atmosphere.

Mr. Blake transformed the Place 2 B into a family run establishment which has been used by the community over the years to not only raise money for various Charities e.g. the Macmillan Nurses but also in the bringing together of local people, to this end he asked me to supply the staging for the events that he promoted using his profile to highlight local events and good causes.

It shocks & saddens me that a favour to one of his employees has turned out this way, this was not a routine occurrence as there was never any trouble that escalated into violence during his time there that I can recall

Yours Faithfully

Paul Hobday
Managing Director

42

17 August 2009

Mr Ashley Blake
4 Roman Place
Sutton Coldfield
B74 3FJ

Dear Ashley

Your misdemeanor!

I have been following the events of the above and I would like to tell you what I personally
feel about the situation.

Many times I have watched your presentations on BBC Midlands and have been impressed
with your style, gentle, not over professional, never self-important and generally coming
over as a person who cares about the subject which you have presented. I particularly liked
your little wave at the end of your news reading. You never talked down to your audience,
your style was one of informing and helping us to understand rather than the 'I'm superior, I
know it all' manner of some presenters on other channels. We felt that you were there in
our sitting room (as in fact you were) giving us individual attention.

I had an occasion to come face to face with you at my friend's 70th birthday party at 'The
Place 2B' last December. Again I was impressed with your style of dealing with your
customers, professional, unassuming and providing a good service.

From what I have read, like a number of youngsters, you had your fling with things you
were not proud of. What does impress me is the fact that you worked your way out of it to
a successful career and became a valued member of society. I know you must have worked
very hard to achieve that, more so than someone who has it handed on a plate. You are a
great role model for those who think it is never possible.

What really upsets me is the fact that a bunch of rowdy, unruly, badly behaved, selfish
teenagers were able to create the havoc they obviously did and get away with it. I believe
you were only doing what any business person would have done to protect his/her business
and that you were provoked. It must have been very distressing to realise that a party to
celebrate the achievement of maturity from teenager to legally recognised adulthood, can
have turned into such childish arrogant behaviour. I have seen the police programmes on
the TV about what happens with drunken teenagers and am appalled at the young of today.
I would not want to be around when they are 'celebrating' in the way they do, let alone run
a business like you did. I am also rather shocked that parents have not seen the error of the
ways of their offspring.

So, Ashley, I support you and dearly hope that you can come out of this as the shining and
determined person you are. You said when you left the court, 'It's over for me.' I do not
think it is. Friends of mine have the same view as I do so there are a lot of people willing

you on. Look at Jeffrey Archer! He's a survivor! I am sure there is a great deal you can learn from this experience and put it to good use for the future.

At present I work as an IT tutor and everyday I say to my learners, 'Mistakes are not problems, they are an opportunity to learn how to do it better, without making a mistake!' I find the ones who do make mistakes are usually better in the end. It is not enough to be able to do it right first time, if you go wrong you need to understand why. In your case, learn from this experience, your career is not over.

I have said a lot, but I feel that what has happened to you is not insignificant. You have been badly treated by the legal profession. So, I think you deserve us to let you know what our verdict is.

All the very best to you and your partner, Jessica.

Watch this space for your future success.

Yours sincerely

Mary

I was visited by the probation service whose job it was to write about my background and lifestyle, and to assess whether I would be a danger to society. Their report would include a sentence recommendation. My probation officer recommended I receive a suspended sentence. Also during this month I was called into the office to be officially sacked from my BBC job for 'Gross Misconduct', and 'Bringing the BBC into Disrepute'.

The Day of Sentence

Wednesday 2nd Sept 2009

Jess and I were woken by the alarm sounding at 8.00am. I'm a morning person, usually full of optimism, excited to see what the brand new day has in store for me, but that day was an exception, I was in a bad mood and very scared. As soon as I turned my mobile phone on it began to beep constantly with messages of support from friends and colleagues.

We headed off to court arriving at 9.45am to twenty or so snappers, TV crews and reporters. Once inside we were ushered into a consulting room to be briefed by my solicitor and barrister. We talked worst case scenario being eighteen months prison sentence, serve half. Jess began to cry, and I guess it was at that point I knew I wasn't going home with her that day. My briefing was interrupted by the court usher who informed us that due to the amount of media and public interest we had to move to a bigger court room. As I entered I was led to the dock at the back of the court room in which Steve my regular customer, and now co-defendant, was already waiting. We made eye contact but we didn't speak.

The press bench where I'd often sat was packed. I made eye contact with former colleague and friend Giles Latcham, he gave me a friendly wink with his left eye. The hearing lasted for one and a half hours. The judge dealt with Steve first giving him thirteen months in prison for assaulting a young man outside my restaurant. I thought, well if he's got thirteen months and he started the whole incident then I'm likely to get half that. The judge turned to me and after a long speech for the purpose of ensuring the press got the quotes needed for their story, he sentenced me to two years. Although I was shocked I showed no emotion, I tried to get Jess's attention as I was being handcuffed and led away, but the news for her was taking it's time to sink in, she seemed to be in total shock as did the public gallery and the press bench. I mouthed the words 'I love you' to Jess before being led down the steps at the back of the dock. She did the same. I guess I felt a sense of relief that at least it was all over, this was day one of my new life.

* * *

I'm taken to the cells beneath the court, all sorts of paperwork is completed and my belongings taken off me. It's an extremely busy place. I'm placed in a holding cell and told I'll be going on the next available transport. While waiting I'm visited by Kevin and John, inmates at Hewell Grange prison in Redditch. Nice chaps who spend the next hour explaining what is happening to me and what to expect from prison life. It all seems very surreal, everything has blurred edges as though I'm dreaming. I'm snapped out of the daze by being handcuffed to a Reliance officer who leads me onto the bus, meat wagon, Black Maria, whatever they call it but it certainly isn't a bus. I'm led into a tiny compartment within the 'bus' there's just enough room to fit my knees in. I'm released from my shackles and the door is locked. There's a window with a view of freedom, although it's darkened. I keep quiet while others are being loaded on.

Prisoners begin shouting comments. They've seen me board the bus and they're shouting to each other and on occasions directly to me,

"Welcome to the real world, welcome to the other side of life, you're gonna be popular in the Green." They sound very intimidating and I'm pleased they can't get to me, they're scary.

As the *bus* pulls away from the Crown Court, photographers attack each darkened window, flashing bulbs send the prisoners into an excited frenzy. Just when I think they've gone I look up and bang, the snapper has the money shot, me in a prison van. The gravity of the situation I'm in begins to sink in and I feel as low as I ever remember.

The journey from the City Centre to Winson Green takes no more than fifteen minutes. It's a familiar route. I know these roads well. Just across the road from the prison is the first house I bought twenty years ago. It was a traditional two up two down, terraced house I'd bought from a housing association back in the days when I had my whole life to look forward to. It was a nice enough house to bring up my newborn son Calam, but we were burgled five times in two years. Twenty years later, I'm back, this time on the other side of those high walls I had spent so much time wondering at. I can't help but feel an irony. Once at *The Green* I am processed into the system, stripped of my identity, I am no longer Ashley Blake, *Blake* will be my name from now on. Steve, my co-defendant and I are kept together and placed in a cell on D Wing, the very same cell notorious Gloucester serial killer Fred West hanged himself in on 1st January 1995.

The Green

Thursday 3rd Sept 2009

I am woken up at 7.30am. There's a constant stream of visitors. The Nurse, the Chaplain, the drugs workers, education department, and so on. Whilst being processed into the system I don't really understand what all these people are saying, everything is still very confusing, I guess I'm still numb from the shock of what is happening to me.

3.15pm we're told to pack up the few things we've managed to accumulate so far, we're being moved to N wing. When we arrive, Steve and I are moved into cell N1-16. The cell is filthy, but it is bigger than the previous one and has a much bigger window at eye level which looks out onto the exercise yard, across from that, some greenery, provided by a large tree just the other side of the perimeter wall. We settle in as best we can. After twenty minutes the door is unlocked and we're told to report to the classroom on the fourth floor. As we arrive we are greeted by half a dozen inmates all wearing green trousers who tell us to take a seat. It is their job to conduct an induction, we are told how the wing works, any problems they are our first contact, not the officers. I learn that these inmates are known as cleaners and *Listeners*. They hold a privileged position on the wing, trusted by officers to keep the wing running as smoothly as possible meaning less work for them, presumably.

The evening is spent with Steve and I watching TV and chatting, reflecting on our situation.

HMP BIRMINGHAM
IN CELL TELEVISION
PRISONER AGREEMENT

You are being provided with in cell television (subject to availability). The cost for this is 50p per week. This will be deducted from your spending account on a weekly basis. In advance and is non refundable. Even if you are on D wing for one day you will be charged the 50p. If you do not agree you will be placed in a cell without a television.

You are responsible for the equipment in your cell. If you cause any damage, adapt or misuse the equipment or tamper with the security seal you will be placed on Governors Report and the privilege will be withdrawn.

You must : ensure the television remains in your cell at all times and is not to be loaned out to anyone. Keep the volume to a reasonable level and turn the set off when you are not in your cell and by midnight at the latest. The equipment remains the property of HMP Birmingham and will not go with you when you are moved to another wing, transferred to another prison or discharged.

In return, we expect your behaviour to reflect the privilege that you have been given with the in-cell television. If your behaviour falls below the standard you may have the privilege of having a television removed.

We expect the following: no lines, no shouting out of your cell window, no rubbish to be thrown out of your cell window, a tidy and clean cell a all times, excess kit to be placed in the correct containers in the recess, no pornographic pictures to be displayed on your cell walls and finally up and dressed by 07.45 hrs.

IN CELL TV IS NOT A RIGHT IT IS A PRIVILEGE

Friday 4th Sept 2009

I've been here for two nights and so far things have gone better than I expected. Steve and I have been supporting each other and it has been strangely exciting in a scary, not knowing what's going to happen next, kind of a way. The cell door is unlocked at 1.47pm, to my surprise an officer tells me I have a visitor. Great, my first visit is my girlfriend Jess and my sister Abi. I'm so pleased to see them both, though I'm conscious I look a mess. A broken man, unshaven, un-showered, wearing prison clothing and a high-vis' vest for visiting purposes. I worry that if Jess is going to see me this way, it'll be easier for her to leave me for someone new. After-all, who would blame her? The paranoia of prison is already setting in.

The visit goes well but we're all fighting back the tears and working so hard to stay positive. Two hours we get to spend with each other but it feels more like five minutes. I have mixed emotions when Jess leaves, I want to break down and cry but I am also so happy to see her and for her to see that I am doing ok, but inside I am not. She worries about me so much. They say it's often worse for the people on the outside, not knowing what's going on. I return to my cell and although I was happy to see her I gradually fall into a deep depression.

Saturday 5th Sept 2009

Twenty-three hours locked away, more potatoes for lunch and dinner.

Sunday 6th Sept 2009

Twenty-three hours spent in the cell reading graffiti and chatting to Steve.

Monday 7th Sept 2009

Apply for emergency credit to use the phone. A letter arrives from Jess

Tuesday 8th Sept 2009

Another boring, non-eventful day locked up for twenty-three hours.

Wednesday 9th Sept 2009

One week in, door's unlocked at 8.30am. My cell mate Steve, is told to pack his things he's being transferred. Forty-five minutes later he's gone. HMP Walton in Liverpool is his destination I am alone for the first time since arriving in prison. It is strange, we've been stuck together for the past week and although Steve will never be my ideal roomy we've helped each other cope with this new life experience, the first week in jail. In fact, I really don't know how I'd have got through it without his familiar face every day. We've recounted funny stories about events that have happened over the years at the restaurant, we've gossiped about mutual friends, we've spoken openly about our feelings, we've shared things we would never have shared in normal circumstances, private things only a situation like this could bring out. But he's gone now and I can't help but feel sadness. I've lost the one and only friend I have in this hell-hole. He's never really been a close friend but he's the one and only connection to my life on the outside - the life I so desperately miss.

Alone in the cell I begin to worry about who my next cell mate is going to be. A smack-head, a filthy person, a stranger? We won't get on, he'll want to know all about me. I'm worried.

At 10.30am the cell door is unlocked, it's exercise. I walk out onto the yard alone when it would normally be with Steve, we'd often break off to talk to other inmates, but there was a certain reassurance that we were always looking out for each other. This time, however, he's not there, I realize I'm feeling very vulnerable. When exercise is over I mention to Officer Skitt that I feel vulnerable and ask about the chances of getting a single cell. He informs me that I do not hold single cell status, this is usually reserved for people with severe mental issues, which they tend to take out on their cell buddy by beating them up. Therefore, nothing can be done for me. I'll be having a new pad mate before long. Officer Skitt comes back a short time later, according to him during our earlier conversation I'd used a trigger word which caused him some concern, the word was 'vulnerable'. He wants to reassure me that if I have any problems then I am to tell him, and it is his job to look after me. He also offers me a place on P Wing which is highly protected from general inmates because it houses 'nonses' and paedophiles. I respectfully decline his kind offer. A few more boring hours go by watching daytime telly when I hear the now familiar sound of jangling keys nearing my door. As the key slides into the lock on my door I think, 'here we go, I'm about to meet my new cell mate'. It is Mr. Jones a very pleasant officer with a great sense of humour. He asks whether I want a job.

"Of course" I say, anything's better than sat here watching daytime TV. He tells me to grab what little stuff I have, and to move onto the 4's. That's the floor at the top of this wing where all the wing cleaners are housed.

I move in with a guy called Gareth. He's been here for two weeks already. He's been sentenced to three and a half years for intent to supply Class A drugs. He was arrested with 16 grams of coke which he tells me he was dealing to close friends. It was his first offence and he feels his sentence was too harsh. He like me, has also lost everything, a good job and a good reputation. We instantly get on well, he seems kind and generous and easy to get along with, I think we're going to be all right here, we'll be fine.

I settle in and we choose to turn out the lights around midnight, I lie awake for quite some time thinking about all sorts, Jess mainly. Then Gareth begins to snore! The single most annoying sound known to mankind. As it gets progressively louder I start to think; "My punishment is my loss of liberty, but this is like Chinese torture!" After an hour or so I ask whether he can do anything about his snoring, half asleep he apologizes and falls silent - for twenty minutes before coming back with a vengeance. The night is the worst night so far, spent shouting at Gareth to stop him snoring.

Thursday 10th September 2009

It's my 8th day in prison. After an awful night's sleep with my new cell mate Gareth who I spent the entire night shouting at to stop snoring, I start my new job. I'm shown how to sweep the No.2's landing and then how to mop it. The whole job takes no more than twenty minutes, but it feels good to be out of the cell and doing something - it beats watching Jeremy Kyle hands down, and for that I am grateful.

I make enquiries to move cells, I can't face another sleepless night listening to Gareth's snoring. I am kindly offered to bunk in with Sunil two cells along. An Asian lad, who's well educated after attending a number of boarding schools. He's on remand for conspiracy to import six million pounds of drug from Holland. We hit it off immediately and we're soon chatting at length about life's experiences. He's twenty-four years old and wants to be a millionaire by the time he's thirty. We spend an hour or so in a *getting to know you* type of conversation, at the end of which it's obvious we're going to get along very well.

After another mouth-watering lunch of boiled potatoes, faggots and peas, one of my favourite dishes on the outside, I am invited to attend the gym with my fellow cleaners, my new colleagues. Attending the gym on a regular basis is another perk of my new privileged position. I excitedly agree to attend and the lads put me through my paces to gauge what I'm made of. I haven't attended a gym for a very long time and begin using muscles that have been dormant for years. The small gym is busy with inmates from other wings around the prison. The officers and inmates recognize me immediately and I attract the usual attention with people coming over to confirm that I am that bloke off the TV and to tell me that I look a lot bigger on the telly, the most often said comment people make when meeting me for the first time.

During one particular exercise I am called over to a chap who says;

"You're the bloke that had a row outside your place!" I said I am, to which he replies, with an aggressive look on his face,

"That was my cousin you hit."

I immediately became very worried and reply

"Really? What's his name?" He repeats

"That was my cousin, yeah".

He stares at me as if he wants to rip my head off. He doesn't confirm his cousin's name so I hope he is lying. He says

"I'll see you after, right!" I can show no sign of weakness and decide to front his request with a simple response of

"Yeah, ok, if you like", and then I swiftly move away.

I try to carry on unaffected, and, as though nothing has been said, but I am shitting myself. I keep glancing over to the man that has just threatened me trying not to make eye contact, but to be sure of his movement. I don't want him 'accidentally' dropping a bar-bell on my head. After a short while the threat gets to me and my new colleagues have noticed a change in my mood and begin to work out what is going on. They are great, and reassure me that there is nothing to worry about, we will all stick together and it will be sorted. I can't help thinking that my introduction to the gym is over, if it's going to be like this I'll not be attending the gym for as long as I'm in prison.

It isn't long before I am approached by the friend of the man who threatened me. He is equally as scary looking but his tone of question is much more friendly, and I am happy to answer him in the hope that he can persuade his mate not to beat me up. I notice out the corner of my eye, angry man has seen us chatting and begins to make his way over, I think, 'Shit, here we go', but I also think nothing's going to happen while we're in here in front of my new colleagues and the prison officers surely. Angry man speaks directly to me, and to my surprise this time he is really friendly. He tells me that he was only joking with what he'd said earlier, he was just winding me up. I laugh a huge sigh of relief and say something like

"Yeah, I thought you were just joking".

By this time my new colleagues who've been watching all the time come over to check that I am OK. I am, what a relief. Turns out angry man goes by the name of Kieran Cairns from Northfield in Birmingham, and his friendly friend is John Owen. I promise to mention them in this book, so here it is, knee caps saved!

Of course I am relieved that my first encounter of bullying behind bars is nothing more than a wind up, but it has left me wondering just when the real deal is going to happen.

Wednesday 16th Sept 2009

I wake this morning in a really bad mood, hardly surprising you'd think! The worst mood I've been in since arriving. It is, I guess, because it is my two week anniversary and I've felt every second of it.

When you go on holiday two weeks flies by and before you know it you're back at the coalface, but here the past two weeks have dragged, it's been truly dreadful.

My first visit of the morning is by two officers who want to carry out a random drugs test on me. They require me to produce a urine sample of around two centimeters. Trouble is I've just got out of bed and emptied the contents of my bladder enjoying the relief as one does first thing in the morning. So this means I am unable, at this precise time, to provide the officers with the required measurement. Despite them running the water in the sink constantly. I explain my inability to provide, they understand and leave saying they'll be back within the hour. Thirty minutes pass and I've consumed two cups of prison tea in an attempt to adhere to the random drugs testing team's requirements. By this time the wing is a hive of activity with my new colleagues busily painting walls just outside my cell. The officers return, hand me a beaker and demand I produce enough urine in order for them to complete their test. The pressure is on, tap running, I concentrate hard, imagine waterfalls, imagine bursting to go, but nothing comes. One officer says

"Looks like we're gonna be here for a while doesn't it Blake?"

Then he takes a seat next to my pad mate at the back of the cell and lights a cigarette. They begin chatting and watching TV. So, here's the scene; one officer is sitting, chatting with my cell mate, the other officer is stood by the cell door which is open and is right next to the toilet, I'm now in full view of anyone on the landing. One lad shouts

"It's the first celebrity prick I've seen!"

The pressure is too intense and now I'm feeling as though they think I've something to hide. I try to explain again, but I am told in no uncertain terms that it if I fail to provide a sample within the next eight minutes then I will be deemed to have failed the drugs test and marked as positive. The pressure intensifies, I make more tea, drink more water, and at last, just before my allotted eight minute deadline, I am able to provide. I fill the tiny beaker to the point where it begins to overflow, I hand it to the officer and continue my flow into the toilet bowl. He dips his test kit into the beaker and by the time I've finished peeing the test is complete and I am handed a certificate as a reward for providing a negative drugs test. I will hang this certificate next to the awards I've received for television journalism. It's a keeper. From then on the day gets better, although I can't stop peeing!

HM PRISON SERVICE
Public Sector Prisons
BIRMINGHAM

This is to certify that

CN7762 BLAKE

has provided a
negative
Voluntary Drug Test
result
on

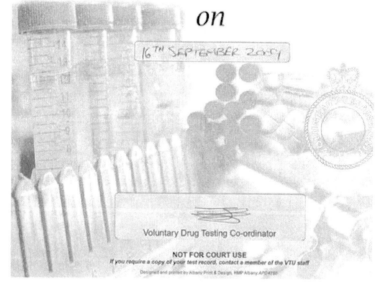

16TH SEPTEMBER 2009

Voluntary Drug Testing Co-ordinator

NOT FOR COURT USE
If you require a copy of your test record, contact a member of the VTU staff

Designed and printed by Albany Print & Design, HMP Albany APD4790

68

Saturday 19th September 2009.

I wake at 8.30, a lie in at weekends. My first job on the ground floor is to sort large black dustbins full of used towels and dirty bed linen, smelly t shirts, socks and filthy boxer shorts. My job is to sort them and bag them for delivery to the laundry. Although I am wearing yellow rubber gloves it is a pretty disgusting, smelly job. The bins stink of sweaty socks and God knows what is in those boxer shorts, I try not to look, but at times can't help catch a glance as I unravel those that are tangled. I bag the sorted piles of dirty washing hoping that when they reach the laundry someone will take the decision to burn rather than wash them.

9.30am
I can wait no longer to speak to Jess so I ring and wake her up. She tries to sound as though she's been awake for ages, but I know her too well. It is, as always, great to hear her voice. She tells me that she's been out with the girls the night before, and I can't help but feel envious and worried, but I don't let on. She is reluctant to tell me that she's been out, but I tell her to live her life and not to put it on hold because of me.

69

She says she's spent most of the night crying and talking about me before going home early. I remind her to live her life, but not to kiss any boys. I'm convinced it will happen during my time inside, but I try hard not to think about it. Prison paranoia is spreading like a cancer around my brain.

The next call I make is to my best friend Gez. I haven't spoken to him since we went for farewell drinks during the August Bank Holiday just before I was sentenced. It is great to talk to him. He is surprised to hear my voice and struggles with what to ask me first. I reassure him that I am doing all right, and the conversation continues as though I'll be seeing him later today for a beer. As I come off the phone I struggle to hold back the tears, it's the first time I've felt the overwhelming urge to cry since arriving in prison.

I begin to miss my life. My eyes redden and I head for a shower to mask my blarting. I battle to pull myself together, I can't let anyone see me crying, it's a sign of weakness in here and I'd be sure to pay the consequences if I'm caught. I eventually pull myself together, enough to return to my cell where Sunil is always able to provide a conversation to help take my mind off things.

Sunday 20th Sept 2009.

I wake at 8.30 again today. I do a little of the usual work of gathering and sorting prisoners dirty laundry. During an hour of the day called 'Association', which is the part of the day where inmates are unlocked for an hour to socialize, make phone calls and shower, I am asked by someone to cut their hair. Always happy to help, I agree. It is a simple enough job using clippers, and the guy simply wants the whole lot off, easy. However, as the cutters near the scalp they reveal a severe dose of dandruff, the worst I've ever seen. It is so bad I begin to feel nauseous, but I can hardly stop half way through. I persevere to the end and he is happy with the result. I don't hang around to be thanked and run to the hot water dispenser to scrub my hands until they are raw. I'll not be cutting anyone's hair from now on. I wake Jess up with a phone call just after 10am. As always it is great to hear her voice. I take a walk around the exercise yard which is sixty foot square. The autumn sun is warm, and I sit down to soak it up. My thoughts soon begin to turn to home, I imagine what I'd be doing right now if I was there. A pint of Guinness and the Sunday papers, my usual Sunday past-time.

Sunday lunch today is pork, potatoes and something purporting to be vegetables though what sort, I'm not sure. A treat comes in the shape of a chocolate muffin and custard for dessert. This is about as good as the food gets in here. After lunch the doors are locked for an hour or so.

2.30, I call Jess for the second time today, she sounds really down and has a headache. I'm not there to look after her I think. We chat briefly and then she is gone. The all too familiar feeling of depression consumes me as soon as the call is over. Rather than return to the cell I stroll to the far end of the landing to a large window which looks out onto the exercise yard and the perimeter fence. I am more interested in the view beyond that where I can see five large trees, their leaves are just turning colour. The view offers glimpses of the outside world. In the park I can see people walking their dogs, youngsters kicking a ball, I can see a taxi reversing around a corner on the adjacent road, all very normal, everyday things but these simple views are views of freedom which have been taken away from me. It feels strange, very strange indeed. My depression deepens, after two and a half weeks in here the initial excitement and fascination has worn off. I decide I have to stop myself thinking about my life outside. Every time I talk to Jess I have the same feeling of an overwhelming depression of what life was, but it's a call I will continue to make. Time spent talking to Jess is so valuable to me and I'm sure it is to her.

Monday 21st Sept 2009.

Monday starts at 7.27a.m. A very quiet morning with nothing much happening. Still feeling quite down but better than when I went to bed last night. Watch TV for much of the morning, write a letter to Jess. Have a meeting with a guy called Richard who's from some training company. He assesses me for any type of job or education I may need, all part of the rehabilitation process. He soon realizes that my need for formal education is a no go, and asks me whether there's anything I'd like to do that he could help with. I mention that I had begun flying lessons and ask whether he can arrange for my ground school books to be sent in so I could continue the theory part at least. He will see what he can do. I return to my cell to find the post has been delivered, a letter from my former producer, Naomi Bishop, it is great to hear from her. My letter reading is interrupted by a new inmate banging on his cell door and shouting at the top of his voice. The noise echoes around the entire wing upsetting inmates locked in other cells who begin protesting at his annoying behavior. The banging inmate soon attracts the attention of an officer who denies whatever request the inmate has made which makes him become even louder with his banging. After a short while I hear the officer giving his cell number to a neighbouring prisoner, I learn that by doing so the annoying prisoner will be dealt with by his neighbours as soon as the doors are unlocked on the next occasion. The last time this happened was during the early hours of the morning. The entire wing was woken up by what sounded like a screaming banshee. When a female officer went to the offending cell to investigate the commotion the inmate spat in her face. When she was asked by other inmates which cell was making the noise she gladly offered the information. As soon as the doors were unlocked the very next morning the screaming banshee was attacked, punched twice full in the face bloodying his nose and no doubt cracking a few teeth. Punishment for waking the wing during the early hours.

Tuesday 22nd Sept 2009.

7.45a.m. I am awake thinking about the incident that led me to being imprisoned and how the trial went, They are the usual thoughts I've been desperately trying to avoid thinking about, it just angers me when I do. I'm in better spirits today. Speak to Jess at 8.30am to wish her a good day. Then go for a stroll once the gates are unlocked for exercise. A George Best lookalike entertains the crowd by stripping down to his boxer shorts and completing a victory lap of the yard much to the amazement of the lads and an inquisitive group of officers. Whilst *George* is enjoying the attention, his mate rolls up his clothes into a ball before rugby kicking it to the top of the security fence where the bundle of clothes becomes entangled on the razor wire. The scene is hilarious to watch as the naked old fella is taken away by a group of officers, I laugh a laugh that feels so strange as I haven't laughed for weeks. My first laugh.

The afternoon is spent in the gym running on the treadmill followed by a game or two of badminton. It feels good to exercise and comes as a relief.

I spend the evening trying to convince my young pad mate not to attack Gareth. Gareth, you recall, is my ex-cell mate who snores. There's a personality clash between the two and a few of the other cleaners. Gareth seems to rub them up the wrong way but he doesn't deserve to be bullied, no one does. I hope my advice to Sunil works but I can't help but feel for Gareth and I decide to play mediator as best I can.

Wednesday 23rd Sept 2009.

My day starts at 7.30am by folding four hundred bath towels which have been delivered freshly from the laundry room. Not the most brain taxing work but at least I am out of my cell. Talking of which, my cell is twelve feet by eight feet. There is a bunk bed with solid mattresses and hard pillows. There's a flushing toilet, unscreened, in the corner, next to that is a sink with push button hot and cold water. The window is quite large, one by one meter, it's double glazed with perspex and steel bars. There are vents providing fresh air instead of opening windows.

I spend the morning looking forward to 2.00pm., I have a visit from Jess booked and I can't wait to see her.

2.00pm.
It is great to see Jess today although I am upset to hear she's been to see friends at a certain lap-dancing club they own in the centre of Birmingham. I am upset she's put herself in a position where men may feel they could take advantage of her vulnerable situation. We've been all over the papers and on the TV for the past nine months, and people will know I'm in prison and unable to be with her. Jess assures me that she is OK, but understands my concern. She hits me with another bomb-shell, she's planning to work for the lap-dancing club organizing gentlemen's lunches in the run up to Christmas. I share my concerns with that idea and tell her I don't want her to work in that industry at all. Our conversation brings more bad news, my car has been repossessed, my debts are mounting up. I

can now understand why Jess is considering taking the job. We need the money.

It is so sad to see her leave, I won't be seeing her again for another ten days, she's not even out of sight and I begin to miss her.

I spend the rest of the day thinking about her news and I'm concerned she'll go ahead and take the job in the lap dancing club anyway, but just not tell me, after all there's no way of me knowing. It's a common feeling among prisoners who each day look at their partners' photos and wonder what they are doing, or who they're with. This is the ultimate test of trust. I wonder whether we'll make it?

Thursday 24th Sept 2009.

Awake at 7.27am after a dreadful night's sleep. For the past five nights an alarm bell in the distance begins to ring at 9.00p.m., and continues throughout the night until 7.00a.m, it's like a form of torture. Needless to say I'm not in the best of moods and I decide that I will give the gym a miss today, however, my cell mate Sunil is having none of it and persuades me to go. I play badminton and feel much better for it, bad mood gone. I call Jess who's been speaking to my agent about managing publicity. Jess also tells me that I'm on the front page of the evening paper again, this time the story is about Staffordshire University may be stripping me of my honorary doctorate.

Friday 25th Sept 2009.

Up at 7.46a.m. Begin to work by emptying and sorting the dirty laundry bins. This is cut short by an officer ordering us all back to our cells. Turns out an inmate has gone missing. We spend the rest of the morning banged up while officers tally the numbers.

Saturday 26th Sept 2009.

A long, boring day and an even more boring evening. My pad mate takes control of the TV, choosing to watch his favourite film *The Lord of The Rings*, followed by two lots of football. I am not interested in either and it isn't my idea of Saturday night entertainment. I take my frustration out on him by playing a very childish game, fighting with rolled up magazines. The game becomes serious when I catch him with a great shot full in the face. He is intent on revenge and therefore the 'game' goes on for some time, we are sweating profusely and decide to call a truce. I lie awake listening to Match of The Day and the distant alarm bell. Sleeping in jail is like entering a torture chamber. I contemplate trying to get a single cell. Would it be better if I were on my own where I could watch what I like, when I like, or would I become lonely with only my thoughts for company. Sunil is the perfect pad mate, our short friendship has become very good but we're beginning to take our frustrations out on each other. Perhaps I should make efforts to get a single cell.

Monday 28th Sept 2009.

I'm woken at 7.30am. I wake in much the same way as I have for most of this year, as if from a nightmare. It takes just a few seconds before the full realization of where I am sinks in and I become overwhelmed with a depression which is unshakeable. Having never suffered depression before it's difficult for me to compare it to anything I've experienced in the past. I attempt to prevent myself from being miserable by turning my thoughts to the future. I think about Jessica waiting for me and I look forward to being with her again, tidying up after her, cooking for her, cuddling her and sharing our thoughts and worries with each other, you know the usual things loving couples do.

The morning continues with work and before long I'm up to my elbows in dirty laundry. My first job is to separate filthy boxer shorts from smelly socks, bag them for the laundry room where they'll receive a boil wash, one hopes. This is followed by dirty towels, jumpers, sheets and blankets. The stench is enough to make me retch and I daren't look at what I'm doing for fear of seeing something that will lead to a full evacuation of my stomachs contents.

10.30am, we're invited to take exercise which consists of walking in circles around a sixty by sixty foot yard encased by a twenty foot high mesh fence on top of which is looped razor wire. Beyond that a slightly higher solid wall. During my walk I begin to chat with a new face. Paul is an intelligent twenty-four year old who was a bar manager, but is now facing a couple of years behind bars for insurance fraud. We discuss our thoughts of prison so far and decide that once this sentence is done, we won't be coming back, ever.

I've been here for twenty-eight days now and I've been advised to apply for "Enhanced status". To clarify; there is Basic, Standard and Enhanced status. When you arrive at prison everyone is considered as Standard, which entitles you to a certain level of standard privileges. According to the prison service's official induction manual;

The prison operates a system of incentives and earned privileges in which there is an opportunity to achieve an enhanced level.

The purpose is to encourage responsible behaviour and encourage inmates to show effort in education, work and other constructive activities, to create a controlled, disciplined and safe environment for all, and to promote and encourage a drug free environment.

To maintain this Standard level of privileges a prisoner must be polite and respectful, no misuse of drugs, co-operate with drug testing, positive use of all offered regime activities, and show respect for establishment rules and regulations. Again taken from the official induction manual. Basic prisoners are assessed every four weeks and have specific targets to help them progress up to Enhanced. However, if an inmate misbehaves then it is possible to be dropped to "Basic" and therefore a loss of Standard privileges.

Having checked the criteria I am confident I'll be a suitable candidate for promotion, my main motivation being an entitlement to one extra visit from Jess per month. So I begin the process of completing an application for consideration for Enhanced status. This involves attaining two references from prison officers, and an explanation of why I feel I'm entitled to a promotion.

I seem to be smoking more each day. I had given up shortly after arriving in prison, but my generous cell mate Sunil offers me a roll-up each time he has one and I accept his kind offer, amounting to around five a day. I feel any little pleasure to help me through this nightmare is worth it.

Prison isn't as bad as I thought it would be, and I certainly do not think it's a deterrent.

The worst thing is the obvious loss of liberty, not being able to see loved ones when you want, but although the day to day routine is monotonous, I have little responsibility and nothing to worry about like paying bills for example. I get three meals a day which I don't have to buy or cook myself, I don't even have to wash up afterwards, if I didn't know any better, then it's not a bad way of life. As for the accommodation, I'm on a wing which was built only five years ago and therefore, is quite modern compared to the rest of the jail, I've certainly paid good money to stay in worse places. For many prisoners, jail offers a better standard of living than they would have on the *out*. There's an opportunity to get an Open University degree while in here. It would be much cheaper to go to prison to get a degree. Here the course is paid for, the accommodation is free, three square meals a day, no utility bills and you actually get paid for doing the course! I just do not understand this system, where's the punishment. Students are struggling with increasing fees and huge debt but not at the university of criminality, HMP UK. I've learned that it costs the tax payer around £100 per day to keep me here. I fail to see any benefit of that. My punishment has already been served with the loss of my career with the BBC, one that I had spent years working so hard on and was so passionate about. I realize that the justice system needed to punish me but surely it would have been better to give me a community service order where I'd be making some sort of contribution to society rather than it costing society to keep me here.

Today I have decided to believe in fate. I haven't always, but too many things have happened to me which are inexplicable at the time and have seemed to send me down the right path. Strange I know, but bear with me. So I'm left with the notion that what is meant to be will be. I have been racking my brains to try to work out why this has happened to me, what have I done to deserve this? What am I supposed to do with this experience? On one hand it's exciting, I guess it will all become clear in the fullness of time. What I have learned already is that I'm guilty of taking things for granted. I have a fantastic partner and some fabulous friends. I've always known that, but now I know for certain and I will prioritize them more when I'm out. It feels like being given a second chance. Many people only realize this when it's too late, like for example being diagnosed with a terminal illness. I have the opportunity here to realize it now and to be able to do something about it once I'm free again, so what I do with this experience is extremely important.

I receive a letter from the editor of a major newspaper wanting me to write an article about my experience of prison so far. Given all the publicity surrounding my case lately I'm very dubious about writing anything so decide to ignore the letter and get on with my sentence.

Tuesday 29th Sept 2009.

I am woken this morning at 6.30am. My cell mate Sunil is being taken to court in Nuneaton. I had a decent night's sleep, the alarm bell which has been annoying me for days has stopped ringing. I am half asleep when the cell door is opened and Sunil leaves. I don't have chance to say goodbye or to wish him luck in whatever he is appearing for, we never discussed it. I get up shortly afterwards to see that out of the goodness of his heart Sunil has left me some tobacco and cigarette papers. He is, as I've said before, a generous person and I've learned that he is also thoughtful and considerate too.

At work I sort a few bins of dirty laundry before going to the gym. I play badminton. I am locked up for much of the morning. Lunch today is particularly poor. Baked-potato, beans and two vegetable sausages. I write a letter to Steve Dyson, the editor at the Birmingham Post & Mail newspaper. The subject consists of youths and their anti-social behaviour. It takes the best part of two hours as I am trying to be constructive rather than angry. I decide not to post it as I run the risk of it being printed and my opinions misconstrued. There is a spare place for the gym this afternoon, so I snap it up as a good way of de-stressing after my letter writing. I play badminton again.

When I return I learn that my pad-mate Sunil won't be coming back to Winson Green, he's been taken to Blakenhurst on the outskirts of Birmingham. I am so disappointed with the news, I'm alone in my cell again.

I speak to Jess for the first time today at 6.15pm. She sounds very pissed off and I'm not able to look after her, it upsets me. The conversation is cut short, officers decide it's early bang-up and we're locked behind our doors at 6.30pm.

I'm in the cell on my own tonight for the first time since coming inside and it's lonely, I try hard not to think about stuff. At least with a cell buddy you're able to keep each other occupied with conversation or games, as juvenile as some might be. Sunil was great company and had already become a good friend. His father is in the next door cell and he's more upset than I am. He has the worry of his only son in prison somewhere else and he doesn't have the reassurance of seeing him each day. I usually enjoy my own company, but in here it's very different. I recall last weekend when Sunil had overall control of the telly and I was considering a single cell would be better, how wrong I was. I need to be careful what I wish for. My hope is that I'm just being over sensitive and I will soon get used to being on my own.

Wednesday 30th Sept 2009.

I wake at 7.45am. I've hit the four week mark today, has it gone quickly? Has it hell, I've felt every ticking second. Last night was the first night I'd spent on my own since arriving in prison and despite my earlier reservations it was actually very nice being alone, I prefer it. I work in the store room for most of the morning sorting freshly laundered T shirts, towels and socks. My colleague Downy, serving six years for violence brings his radio in, so we fold and sort to the tunes of commercial radio, a nice treat as I haven't listened to a radio for a month.

I was offered a job in the gardens today. It sounds great but then I thought with winter fast approaching perhaps the gardens won't be the best place. The job is considered to be one of the plum jobs within the prison but it would mean moving wings and getting to know a whole new set of inmates. I seek advice from Miss Ellis, Mr. Jones and Raj senior, Sunil's dad, who all advise me against it and so I turn it down. I get the impression the officers quite like having me around, they've all been very nice to me and I get on well with them. Word of my job offer soon gets round to other officers and my new colleagues who all make it known that they do not want me to go. It's nice to be wanted.

I received a bunch of letters this evening including one from Mark Gough from ITV Central News, it reads:

Just a wee note, I hope you're doing ok. I think most people were surprised at the sentence. Take it easy, Mark.

A short, but very kind note which I much appreciate.

Speak to Jess, she tells me that she'll be coming over to organize my daily newspapers with the local news agent. This means she'll be just the other side of the perimeter wall, in distance it's just a few yards away but in prison terms she may as well be on another planet.

I try to learn the art of rolling a cigarette, it's a case of having to as Sunil is no longer here to do it for me. I'm smoking more now, it's the only bit of enjoyment I seem to get these days. I watch TV for the rest of the evening flicking between the five channels before spending a second night on my own. It is ok, although I do have a moment while watching 'The Secret Millionaire' on C4. A tear comes to my eye as a chap gave away tens of thousands of pounds to good causes. I long to be in the position again to be able to raise money to help others less fortunate, something I did when I was considered a celebrity, and something I look forward to doing again in the future.

Thursday 1st Oct 2009.

Wake at 7.50am and go straight to work. I see another part of this huge prison today on a trip to the laundry department. It is like being given a guided tour by the officer, Mr. Kane. Workers in the laundry department seem pleased to see me though, they also appear to be a little shocked.

Another bunch of letters are delivered to my cell, Nick Owen my colleague and mentor from BBC *Midlands Today* and former *TV am* presenter has taken the trouble to pen a few words. It is great to hear from him. Over the years he's become a good mate and his letter is full of encouragement. 7.00pm we are banged up.

Friday 2nd Oct 2009.

I am wide awake at 6.47am with a profound thought: When you do anything that makes you well known/famous, when you're good at what you do, you've got to assume as many people like you as hate you.

I'm in an excited mood today, Jess is booked in to visit this morning with my sister Abi and I'm really looking forward to seeing them, though very apprehensive as it's always very sad when they have to leave.

It's great to see Jess and Abi, we have two and a quarter hours together, Jess is well and Abi reports that the family is OK. As soon I return to N wing I fall into the all too familiar depression which isn't helped by today's lunch, baked potato and an excuse for a Cornish pasty with beans, all luke-warm. The rest of the afternoon I spend alone in my cell, reading the paper, watching daytime TV and thinking.

Dinner this evening is beef and onion pie, potatoes, cabbage and carrots. I return to my cell to dine and tears begin to roll down my face, just a few before I get a grip of myself - I miss Jess like crazy and I just need to be with her. I want our life back. Apart from a photo of Jess and me taken at her 26th birthday I won't see her in the flesh for another ten days or so - the thought plays on my mind. This is the downside of having a cell to myself.

I become angry while watching the evening news, the lead story is about anti-social behaviour. A man in Staffordshire was attacked and killed over a bottle of wine the day after my incident. A sixteen-year-old boy and twenty-one year-old man were jailed for life. Youth and anti-social behaviour has been making the headlines during the past week, it is what prompted me to write the letter to the editor of the Birmingham Post & Mail which I still haven't sent yet. It frustrates me and brings back memories of my own situation - how was I supposed to defend myself, my home, my staff, my business from up to thirty drunken yobs? How will I ever understand that?

In the most depressed mood since arriving in jail I decide to call it a day and switch out the light at 10.15pm. However, unable to sleep I lie, thinking about my partner, friends and family, and it's not long before tears are streaming down my face. I attempt to roll and smoke a cigarette to calm down, but it has little effect, I cry myself to sleep.

Saturday 3rd Oct 2009.

I wake at just before 8.30am, the cell is very cold as the first of the autumn winds howl around. I begin work, sorting filthy and very smelly laundry, not a great way to start any day. Officer Jones has arranged for me to collect the newspapers allowing me the opportunity to tour the other wings. What an experience. The other wings of this jail are what you'd imagine a prison cell to look like. The prison is over one-hundred and sixty years old and although the cells have been slightly modified over the decades they still resemble their original architecture. The wings are dark, dank and extremely depressing. There is little natural light anywhere and I'm told rats and cockroaches scurry about the landings during the night. N Wing, where I'm housed, is five star in comparison.

The day goes by pretty quickly, at 4.30pm I'm preparing to be banged-up for the night when a young black guy taps on my door. I assume he's here to ask for some *burn*, which is prison talk for a cigarette, but he tells me he's my new cell mate. I'm devastated, I've just gotten used to my own company and luxury of being in a cell on my own, now I'm forced to share the tiny space with a complete stranger. I attempt to prevent him from moving in by asking the prison officers to find him somewhere else, but they are not interested in my protest. So this stranger moves his stuff in and we begin the process of getting to know a bit about each other. He has very few belongings and no tobacco, I am happy to share what little I have with him, along with a few goodies such as chocolate muffins and biscuits I've accrued. He is pleasant enough to get on with and the evening passes watching TV. We agree to switch the lights out at around 11.30pm, shortly afterwards my new cell mate begins to snore. This continues, getting louder and louder as the night gets darker and darker. The noise prevents me from getting even a wink of sleep, and despite shouting and rocking the bunk he continues to snore, seemingly enjoying a sound night's sleep. I look forward to lights out. It marks the end of another day, it's another day closer to going home and when you're asleep you're not in prison your dreams allow you to be anywhere. Tonight, however, I'm very much in prison and I'm also being tortured by being deprived of sleep with the world's most annoying sound. The anger I feel is indescribable as I've never felt it like this before, it's enough to drive someone to murder, or at least manslaughter, on the basis of diminished responsibility. I'm saved from my thoughts of murder by the Japanese Grand Prix live on BBC One at 5.00am. The race breaks the monotony of the noise coming from the top bunk and I hope the noise of Formula One cars racing round will at least prevent him from enjoying a sound sleep as revenge.

The cell door is unlocked at 9.00am and not having had any sleep I am not in the best of moods. I don't hold back during my complaints to a small group of prison officers who are chatting at one end of the landing. To my surprise this time they listen and begin a mass shake up of the 4's landing. This means shifting inmates around, some who are in a single cell are moved into a shared cell, and they are not happy. I feel responsible for the shake up and word gets around that it is because of my complaints. I become concerned and expect to have to pay a penalty for disturbing the status quo, but it is explained by the officers that it is nothing to do with my complaint, and that they are preparing for the Christmas influx of prisoners. Phew!

I get a new cell mate, Paul, who I befriended over the last few days, and we get on very well. Last night's snorer moved in with Gareth the other snorer, great, there is justice!

Sunday 4th Oct 2009.

So, Paul reluctantly moves into my cell, he's upset because he's also been forced to give up the luxury of a single cell. It's not long before I realize my new pad-mate has OCD, Obsessive Compulsive Disorder and he talks for England. He's a nice bloke, who likes to have routine and order in his life, and he immediately begins the task of arranging his belongings into the order of his disorder. I like clean and tidy but this guy takes the meaning to a whole new level. He sets out his personal grooming products in straight lines and there has to be symmetry. His towels and t shirts have to be folded in a certain way, his process takes at least an

97

hour and half but he's still not done, he spends more time making tiny adjustments to whatever he's set out, tiny, little movements to align everything according to how his mind wants it. As I'm writing this entry he's attempting to make the cell as homely as he possibly can, he's covering all the surfaces in blue *J-cloths* to disguise as much of the prison grey Formica as possible. Although I understand his attempts to disguise his surroundings and the reasons for why he's doing it, there comes a point when you have to accept that you're in prison and no amount of decoration will substitute the freedom of your own home. His annoying behaviour soon begins to grate on my nerves, and it highlights just how good my cell mate Sunil was, easy going, funny intelligent, generous, we were very similar in personality and we gelled. I can see this guy becoming a right pain but there is a bonus, he doesn't like football either.

I get the chance to speak to Jess at around 9.30am as she's just arriving at work. I miss her so much. The conversation is brief but it's important I speak to her whenever I get the chance just to hear her voice and to be sure she's okay.

The rest of the day is spent getting to know my new pad mate who's continually arranging and rearranging his small collection of stuff. I begin to understand Paul more as the day goes on, he's a nice bloke who talks non-stop, but perhaps it's his way of coping with the situation.

7pm and I seize the opportunity to call Jess again. She's walking from New Street train station to her Mum's house in Edgbaston, a journey of approximately one and a half miles but it takes her past a few tower blocks and social housing estates. I become upset at her for not taking a taxi as I'm concerned for her safety. She tells me that I'm being over protective and that I'm not to worry - but who can blame me, our luck hasn't been very good lately and it would kill me if anything was to happen to her.

Tuesday 6th Oct 2009.

Up at 7.40am after a decent night's sleep, Paul was a quiet sleeper and apart from feeling his presence in the cell he hardly made a sound. As the door is unlocked I'm told I have a Legal Visit. I'm taken to the visits block where my solicitor Errol is waiting. It's the first time I've seen him since court. He has no news for me, he just wants to see me in the flesh to check how I am coping. He brings me up to date with the appeal and tells me about his Caribbean holiday he's just enjoyed, thanks Errol! The meeting lasts twenty minutes and it is a pleasant change to the morning routine.

Back on the wing my job of sorting dirty laundry had already been done by a colleague allowing time for me to use the phone to call Jess. We speak about my concerns for her safety and that she's to be more aware following all the press coverage, she agrees and promises she'll take more care.

Wednesday 7th Oct 2009.

Up at 7.30a.m., go to the gym, play badminton. I work in the kit room sorting a delivery of fresh clothing and towels. Spend much of this afternoon watching TV and reading the papers. I am given an addition to my job; the Governor wants to know exactly how many inmates are taking showers during association. There are four landings with around forty inmates on each. The shower room consists of four showers, I count only nine people out of a possible forty on my landing who take showers.

My cell door is left open for much of the day and we are ahead with our chores allowing time to socialize with my new colleagues. I am paid a visit by a steady stream of people wanting help with paperwork or just for a chat. It seems I've become the agony aunt of my new colleagues. They come to me to tell me their problems and I help them with a friendly ear an understanding attitude and to articulate their concerns in letters to loved ones and their legal representatives. I'm happy to help, it's in my nature, however, I've become aware of my own welfare, it's okay listening to other people's problems, but how do I cope with my own situation, who do *I* off-load my concerns to? I have to be careful about my open door policy.

Thursday 8th Oct 2009.

Up at 7.50am today. Work awaits in the kit room, I'm on my own there today and quietly get on with sorting piles of clean towels, boxer shorts, jeans and t shirts.

Being alone allows me time to reflect on my situation.

Locked up around 7.00pm, watch telly for the evening, lights out 10.30pm.

Friday 9th Oct 2009.

Day starts at 7.45am with the usual sorting of dirty washing. Off to the gym to play badminton for an hour. The afternoon is spent watching TV. It's Friday so it's early bang up at 4pm.

Saturday 10th Oct 2009.

Today is almost exactly a repeat of yesterday.

Sunday 11th Oct 2009.

Speak to Jess as soon as the cell door is unlocked at 8.30am to remind her how much I love her. I choose to stay in my cell for much of the day chatting to my cell mate who is desperate for a single cell again although we do get on very well. He's decided on a plan to get what he wants, he will make an appointment to see the doctor to complain he's suffering from an OCD condition which is preventing him from going to the toilet in front of his cell mate. I don't believe his plan will work. However, after his appointment later today we're visited by Mr. Matherson who informs Paul that he has received instructions from the doctor and he is on the list for the next available single cell. His plan has worked. I become concerned that I'll have yet another stranger to get to know, unless of course I learn to play by these prison rules and invent a condition which the service has to act upon. I need to learn to play the system.

Monday 12th Oct 2009.

My pad mate Paul insists on getting up at 7.15am for an unknown reason. I'm not one for lying in, however, I try to persuade him that the more hours we spend asleep the less our sentence is. Despite his early rise our door isn't unlocked until 8.52a.m., he's wasted the opportunity of shaving a couple of hours off his sentence by lying in.

Up and about I decide to shave, after lathering up I reach for my Mach 3 Gillette razor, it is missing. Searching the tiny cell takes seconds, my razor is gone, stolen. I cannot believe it. It had cost just £6.99, but that's a lot of currency in here, and someone has just helped themselves to it either for their own use or to use as currency in exchange for whatever. I am upset and disappointed, but soon come to realize that this is, after all, prison and I'm surrounded by thieves.

My loss prompts me to complete two applications: one requesting a transfer to D Category Open Prison, the other for a single cell, it reads;

I have been here for six weeks during which time I have worked hard to fit in well, however, I feel anxious and extremely vulnerable. I have recently been the target of two thefts from my cell and this has led to sleepless nights. Can you please change my status to single cell with immediate effect. I thank you for your consideration in this matter.

This is the start of me learning to play the prison system and within a couple of hours Officer Matherson awards me a single cell due, I'm told, to being a high profile prisoner.

On My Own

N4 - 19, my new cell is so much better, the window offers a view over the perimeter wall towards Birmingham City Centre and freedom as I once knew it. I begin the task of scrubbing my cell from top to bottom and making it as much mine as I can. I use prison issue roll-on deodorant to stick pictures of Jess and family to the walls. Prison issue toothpaste also acts as a suitable adhesive for heavier photos. It's amazing how resourceful one can be in the absence of everyday simple items like glue or sticky tape. Last night I was able to produce a tasty meal of Pilchards and noodles using the tiny travel kettle in our cell. I tipped the Pilchards into the plastic bag which the tea packs come in, placed the bag in the kettle and boiled the water. It was the original boil-in-the-bag and it was great. I also boiled milk in the kettle to make Paul some porridge however, it took an age to scrub the burnt bits off the element afterwards.

Going back to the theft of my razor, I've spent the day casually looking at other inmates who appear distinctively clean shaven! I have my suspicions as to who the thief is but let's face it, in here it could be anyone! If you are he, reading this, then I hope you cut yourself shaving whilst using it you low life piece of shit. Anyway, it has spurred me on to getting my single cell, and I have Mr. Matherson to thank for dealing with it promptly and with a sympathetic understanding. As for my cell-mate Paul, he too secured himself single living space, I'll miss sharing with him and thank you Paul, despite your OCD, we had some great conversations which helped pass the endless hours of frustration, I wish you well.

During the afternoon I am approached by a young lad of around twenty-five years of age asking whether I would help him write a letter to the judge in his case. I agree and, knowing nothing about this chap, I sit down to hear his story. He was arrested for TWOC, Taking Without Owners Consent, and driving without a license. He then tells me it was his girlfriend's car, his girlfriend was also his probation officer and a former prison officer at Winson Green. I write a letter for him with a smile on my face, 'nowt as strange as folk'.

Today doesn't all go well though. I get my first bollocking from officer Kane. A couple of days ago I was asked by a huge black guy called Carl to sign my autograph for him, he presented me with his Cell Card, an official prison document which has a photo of the inmate, how long he's serving and other official stuff. He asked me to write a short message on the back, I wrote:

Nice to meet you while at HMP Birmingham, all the very best for the future, peace and love always, Ashley.

Mr. Kane asked me not to do that, I asked why and he said that it was for prison purposes only. I agree that I won't sign anyone's card again and that was the end of the matter. Kane strikes me as a typical authoritarian, he likes wearing his uniform and he gets a great deal of pleasure out of the position he holds. I've met many like him in my time, traffic wardens usually, need I say more? Miss Walker on the other hand is very caring. I've learned through conversation that she has two teenage sons so she's used to disciplining men and she seems good at her job. During lock up tonight she asks me whether this is my first night alone in a cell, whether I am going to be okay, and whether I've cried yet. I tell her I'll be fine, she closes the door saying "You'll probably have a little cry tonight".

I settle down to watch the new series of the BBC show *Inside Out* I had presented for seven years. It is very strange watching a programme I've fronted for so long being fronted by someone else. Mary Rhodes did a great job, though I naturally can't help feeling that she's stolen my baby. Never did I imagine watching my programme from a prison cell. Needless to say, Miss Walker was right, I do have a cry.

Tuesday 13th Oct 2009.

Awake very early today, it is still dark outside. My door is unlocked at 7.50am and I go straight to the gym for a workout on the running and rowing machines. Back on the wing there isn't much work to be done so I use the time to call Jess. I waste thirty-pence as no one will pick up on my first three attempts. I never thought I'd get so upset about losing thirty-pence, but with very limited phone credit every penny counts. I get through on my forth try, and it is worth it to hear Jess's voice.

Lunch today is jumbo sausage, baked potato and beans. The canteen arrives around 3.30pm, it raises spirits on the wing as everyone has a fresh delivery of much needed treats and tobacco, debts can now be paid, and more deals can be done. I have my first piece of dairy milk chocolate for six weeks which I enjoy whilst reading letters sent in by Jess, my sister Cheryl, Rachel from work, and Nick and Karina, my former airline housemates. It is great to hear from them and I spend the evening replying. Whilst reading the letter from my sister a small plastic credit card size card falls out, it is a poem entitled "Don't Quit". The words are poignant and make me cry. The letter from Nick and his wife Karina contains stories of our time traveling the world together, fond memories of ultimate freedom.

Dinner tonight is chilli and rice, tasteless as usual. There is no association tonight for the wing, except for just the cleaners. It seems strange, this small group of inmates enjoys the privilege of having the wing to themselves, and I appreciate being given the position of a cleaner.

During association inmates are let out of their cells for one hour per day usually between 6 and 7pm. Inmates are allowed to make phone calls, play pool, table tennis, take a shower and mingle with others. association I dislike hugely, it's when I feel most vulnerable. It's also the time when any differences are sorted out so there's usually a fight. Drug deals are done, any thefts from cells take place, and a lot of scrounging goes on. It is the worst hour of my day and I choose to stay behind my door much of the time. I speak to Jess who confirms she's booked in to visit tomorrow. I go to bed looking forward to seeing her and apprehensive about the feeling I'll have when it's time for her to leave again.

Wednesday 14th Oct 2009.

Up at 7.50am and spend the morning working in the stores room sorting kit. Looking forward to Jess's visit this afternoon.

2.00pm and I'm taken to the visits block where Jess is waiting. It is great to see her, full of stories about our wedding plans in Barbados, can't wait! I'm not so sad as she leaves, not that I'm getting used to it, but it doesn't seem so hard to say goodbye this time. Perhaps it's because Jess has done a great job of making me feel much more secure about our relationship by constantly reassuring me of her love and commitment to me.

As I stand with around thirty other inmates waiting to be taken back to our wings a small black guy is the target of the worst violence I've witnessed since I've been here. The black guy was recognized by another as being from P Wing, that's a wing for sex offenders. He denies being from that wing but can't give a convincing answer quick enough. The atmosphere quickly turns, and two inmates set upon him directly in front of me, punching him in the mouth, I hear teeth crack and see blood spilling from between his lips. In the crowded area there isn't much room to get out of the way, the attackers ask others to block the CCTV camera and as they gladly do so they continue their attack, right in front of me. My instinct is to step in and try to calm them down, but that's what I'm in here for in the first place, for getting involved, I

113

could end up much worst off. Despite
screams of help no officers come to assist
the young black man. When a couple of
officers do eventually arrive they are totally
oblivious to anything going on and simply
ask the victim why his mouth is bleeding
before taking him away. Other onlookers
are convinced the officers have deliberately
put the victim in with the main prisoners
knowing that he'll be attacked, something
that often occurs, I'm told!

Sex offenders are usually kept separate from
the rest of the prisoners for their own
safety.

Thursday 15th October

I receive a letter from my biological father
today. He is expressing an interest in
coming to visit me. I write a polite letter
back telling him that I am doing fine, and
that out of the three visits a month I'm
allowed, Jess is the only person I want to
visit me. I also receive a letter from Ian
Winter, sports presenter on BBC *Midlands
Today*. It is great to hear from him. I speak
to Jess at our usual time, around 6.00pm,
she is worried about her job which she has
come to hate. I advise her to resign and

concentrate on promotional work which is a job she really enjoys. As we spend so much time at work, I have never seen the point in doing a job which you hate, the result would be that you spend most of your life miserable, what's the point of that?

Friday 16th October

Cell door is unlocked at 8.30 for my appointment with the nurse for the first of three Hepatitis injections as recommended during my reception to prison. I wait along with around twenty other inmates from different wings in a small waiting room within the hospital wing of HMP Birmingham. The room is like any hospital waiting area, though the obvious differences include steel bars between each door, the glass has been replaced with Perspex, and the windows, which don't open to let in the much needed fresh air, have steel bars. There is a small television high in the corner of the room playing a music channel which can barely be heard above the various conversations that are taking place. I wait as I watch others being called through for their appointment for whatever medical condition they are complaining about. I wait for two hours until 10.30 before being told the nurse hasn't turned up and we are to reschedule. I return to my wing and take the opportunity to phone Jess.

Whilst I have wasted the morning waiting in a sweaty, smelly prison hospital waiting room, back on my wing the canteen forms have been collected for processing. Mine is still lying on my bed. I try to convince officer Skitt to take my form over to wherever they process it. He agrees he will make a phone call. If my form isn't processed it'll mean I will miss out on the all-important weekly shop delivered next Tuesday. Among the items on my list are sweets, chocolate, shaving cream, shower gel and telephone credit to allow me to make my regular daily contact with Jess. All I'm really concerned about is the phone credit, the other items, though luxury, I can live without, not being able to speak to Jess everyday would send me crazy. I decide I will never make the mistake of not submitting my canteen form on time, (Thursday lunch time), ever again.

Today whilst carrying out my cleaning duties, wearing pink rubber gloves, I am stopped by an elderly officer on the stairs. He stares at me for a while then says

"Ashley, I'm sorry to see you in here, you were one of my heroes.", I reply

"Not as sorry as I am.", and we part.

His comment, though nice, gets to me, I feel like bursting into tears right there, right then, partly because I feel this overwhelming sense that I've let him down, and partly because he used the word *were,* as though I've ceased to be his hero anymore. I guess it is the combination of the two that has led me to having to fight the increasing lump in my throat. It sure as hell gets to me for the rest of the day.

Saturday 17th October

Up at around 8.30 this morning, it is the coldest night so far. Not much work to do today, being super-efficient all the cleaners are ahead on our duties, so we socialize. Witness another violent attack. This time four of my new colleagues are involved. They enter a cell and attack a small white guy. The attack lasts no more than a minute or so, and from where I am standing on the landing I can clearly see kicks and punches rain down upon the single occupant. The inmate is struggling with what must be all his strength and survival instinct to get out of the small cell, but he is outnumbered four to one. The scene is like trying to grab hold of a piglet in a pen, and the sound is much the same.

Shouts and whistles alert the four officers on duty who make their way up the stairs from the ground floor. The alarm also alerts the attackers who walk calmly from the scene of their crime before the officers arrive. I later see the victim with no clear signs that he's been so viciously brutalized. I also learn the motive for the attack. It began seven years ago when the victim had burgled the house of his attacker. This was a revenge beating, and provided 'a bit of fun' for the attackers, a release of frustration at being banged up. I speak to those involved a few moments after their attack and they seem relieved and satisfied.

Lunch today consists of chips and a sort of lamb style pasty with tinned tomatoes, though they'd run out of tomatoes. As usual, the offerings are cold and become much colder when it is slopped onto the stainless-steel tray from which we eat all our meals.

I phone Jess at around 1.30pm. It is good to hear her though we don't have much to report. We speak about her choice of a new car, a Saxo, Clio or Corsa. She tells me that she's been at her sisters until late last night. I detect an untruth in her voice, or is it just me being paranoid? I don't pursue it, after all, what can I do if she is seeing someone else, who could blame her? I try to trust her totally, she's given me no reason to distrust her up to now so perhaps I am being over sensitive, silly. Spent the rest of the day reading *Honest,* Ulrika Jonnson's autobiography. Although I've never met her I was surprised when she mentions many of my friends, the late Trisha Williamson, the first weather girl on TV am, Stan Collymore with whom she had a turbulent relationship, and Jeff Berliner one of my colleagues and good friend at BBC *Midlands Today.* Turns out he gave Ulrika her very first presenting job at TV am, you have a lot to answer for Mr. Berliner, no wonder you kept that one quiet in all the time I've known you!
Television is the order of the evening with X Factor then the News, reporting the funeral

of Boyzone's Stephen Gately. Lights out around 11.00pm.

Sunday 18th October

Get up at 8.30, I'm feeling particularly down today, well, actually I've been feeling down for a few days now. I've come down with a cold, nothing too severe at this stage but it's exaggerated by my surroundings. I am asked to sort out the kit room as it is in a messy state. I do the best I can and have it spick-n-span in no time before officer Kane decides to have a wing kit change. Everyone on the wing, around eighty inmates is given the opportunity to exchange their dirty kit for fresh. Within an hour the kit room is a complete mess and I am tasked to begin the cleaning process all over again, this time with pile upon pile of filthy, smelly men's stuff, including boxer shorts, socks and bed sheets. The smell is disgusting.

By the time I've finished, lunch is being served, I don't have much of an appetite having just sorted dirty linen. Roast beef, potatoes (sautéed), and veg, it is the best this week, and it is warm for a change. Dessert is a chocolate chip muffin and the usual Sunday treat of custard. I speak to Jess after lunch who sounds equally as pissed off. We don't have much to talk about so we make the call brief in order to save my phone credit.

I find myself looking out of the window more today. On one occasion in the far, far distance I make out an airplane coming into land at Birmingham Airport. It is a sight I am all too familiar with. My restaurant in Sutton Coldfield was on the flight path to Birmingham Airport, and planes of various sizes used to fly past within a thousand feet or so of the beautifully landscaped garden, providing much entertainment whilst sat out on a barmy summer's evening with my friends and customers. As I look through the window I am instantly reminded of those times until my eyes pull focus to the bars on the windows and back to the reality of the day, I'm in prison, how has this happened to me? It's apparent, I'm falling into a depression, I'm close to tears, I want out of here, I want my life back.

During this evening's association, rather than socialize, I decide to stay in my cell. I read the newspapers, and, using a cigarette rolling machine, I roll as many fags for Raj, my next door neighbour as his stash of tobacco allows. It's a service he's come to rely on me for since his son Sunil was moved to another prison, and I'm happy to oblige.

Monday 19th Oct

Up early today, it remains dark at around 7.20. Still feeling down, but slightly better than at the weekend. Shower and attend an event the prison service has organized entitled 'Black History Month'. I just wrote that as if I was in the normal process of getting ready in the morning and going out to an appointment as millions of people do every day. However, the detail is a lot more restrictive than that and involves being unlocked and let out of the cell, being collected by officers assigned to guard those who have been risk-assessed by the prison security department to be allowed the privilege to attend such an event, and then a two hundred meter walk through various corridors and buildings with no less than twenty gates and doors being unlocked and locked behind us as we make our way to the chapel where the event is taking place.

Once securely inside, there are around fifty other inmates from other wings sat on chairs arranged theatre style in front of a large screen. We are invited to watch a short documentary called 'Bang, Bang In Da Street', by *Rice 'n' Peas* Productions. The film is about gun crime and how black people are portrayed in the media. Within thirty minutes it is over and the assembled audience is asked to discuss the issues. I physically sink in my seat poised for the inevitability of a question being asked directly of me about why the media portray black people in a negative way. A question I don't want to answer as it will require me to use an intellectual explanation and, given the audience, I will run the risk of losing the point and sounding like a big head or figure of authority, something that this group of both black and white men within the age range of 19 to 55 have no respect for.

I respond by saying whoever picks up a gun for whatever reason needs to take responsibility for their actions, the media just stick to the facts of the story whether the person holding the gun is black or white, it is fact that most gun crime in this city is carried out by young non-white men and that is nothing to do with the media being racist. White members of the audience cheer and clap as they consider my answer to be favouring white people. Not my intention. This spurs the debate onto other issues, and it isn't long before I am released from the spotlight, and able to return to being one of them, just another inmate.

During the afternoon I am pleased to receive letters from Jess and two colleagues from the BBC, Sarah Falkland and Dan Pallett. With the cloud of depression still directly above me I lie on my bunk and consume the ever so supportive contents of each letter. Without at first realizing, as I approach the end of each page, I notice the ink has become smudged from the tears falling from my face. I write letters in reply to Sarah and Dan, informing them that despite my predicament I am physically and mentally okay, and thank them for their kind support. The tone of the letters is positive, though I am dying inside. On the way to the post box which is located on the bottom landing, I phone Jess just to hear her voice. She instantly makes me feel better with her unrelenting words of positivity and comfort, I truly love her.

Tuesday 20th Oct.

Up at 7.30am and go through exactly the same procedure as yesterday to attend the second event of 'Black History Week'. Today's screening is about the ripple effect of gun and knife crime, after which guest speakers include Thelma and Barbara, the mothers of sons who lost their lives after becoming involved in gun crime. Also Arthur Ellis the father of Charlene Ellis, who was caught in the cross fire of a drive-by shooting in Perry Barr in Birmingham a few years ago. The discussion is lively but this time I keep quiet and try to observe as much as possible. Thelma, Barbara and Arthur recognize me. I have never met them before but we speak as if we are old friends. They express their disgust at the way I've been treated for what I did, and they wish me well. Their advice is to put it behind me and move forward a stronger person. I promise them that I'll do just that. Our conversation is interrupted by a female prison officer asking for a word with me to one side. She asks whether I'd be interested in joining the prison's race relations committee. My responsibilities would involve regular meetings with prisoners and prison officials regarding any race issues. It sounds very interesting and I agree that it will be of interest to me and I'd be delighted to lend an opinion to any committee, I also think I will be adding something useful to my time behind bars.

During the afternoon I have a backlog of stuff to sort out in the kit room which keeps me busy up until tea-time. I speak to Jess just after six and update her on my new role as race relations rep. Her response is

"Typical, why can't you just do your time and come home?"

She continues to take the piss and advises me not to organize any roof top demonstrations or strikes!

As I retire to my cell the post has been delivered. A letter from a colleague, Debra Mitchell, in which she tells me that she prays for me every day and night, and sends lots of support. I also receive some internal paperwork, information about my possible release dates. My *ERD*, (Earliest Release Date), is 1st September 2010. My *Sentenced To* date reads 1st September 2011, and my *HDC*, (Home Detention Curfew), date is 20th April 2010. Seeing those dates gives me something to aim towards. 20th April is a week after Jess's birthday and I'm hoping to be out by then. HDC works like this; I can be released up to four and half months before the end of my release date on a curfew. I would have to wear an electronic tag and stay in the house between 7.00pm and 7.00am until the 1st September 2010. This is providing that in the meantime I am a model prisoner and cause no issues for concern. I have no intention of doing otherwise and my possible release date excites me. April is still a long way off though and I still have Christmas to contend with first. Nevertheless, it's the trigger I need to move this cloud which has consumed my mood lately and I begin to feel more positive again. Lights out 11.00pm.

Wednesday 21st Oct

Awake at 8.00am. There is no need to get up as it is a prison officers' training day and we aren't unlocked until 11.45am for lunch to be delivered, two small baguettes, a small tub of *dairylea* spreadable cheese, and a packet of instant noodles. An orange provides dessert. It is lucky I had saved two pieces of brown bread from a couple a days ago to make up a suitable lunch, especially as I don't have any personal shopping having missed handing in my canteen request form last week. I receive a card from Hillary McConnell, a fabulous colleague at the BBC, and several other letters from viewers who are very supportive. The afternoon is spent reading and letter writing.

5.30pm we are unlocked for dinner after which I am allowed to call Jess. She's been for an interview and has been offered the position as General Manager at a chain of gyms. I congratulate her, but very much at the forefront of my mind I am feeling insecure. Jess working in a gym, with men obsessed with fitness, surely this could lead to her meeting someone else. Will Jess cheat on me? If she does there'd be no way of me knowing so what's the point of even thinking about it? These are the type of thoughts racing through my over-active, paranoid mind and, no matter how hard I try to stop them, they keep on coming thick and fast, I can do nothing but wait for normal brain activity to resume which, in here, takes much longer than on the outside. Lights out 11.00pm.

Thursday 22nd Oct

Up at 7.45am and catch up with duties missed yesterday, a busy morning followed by lunch. This afternoon attend the third event in 'Black History Week'. Listen to a couple of speakers from a Handsworth based charity called *Bringing Hope*. The presentation is good though lacks any structure, and the nervous speakers keep losing their main point which is to look at your past and decide what you want your future to be. I am impressed as, for the first time this week, we have actually done something about Black History!

Back on the wing not a lot is happening, my cleaning colleagues are chatting to officers and generally milling around. Officer Matherson, who is suffering from the lurgy, gives me a spare sachet of *Lemsip Cold & Flu* as he's noticed I am suffering a little too. It is a kind gesture. He also reminds me to hand in my canteen sheet on time this week, again a kindly reminder.

I make my usual appointment to speak to Jess, around 6.30pm, she is her usual supportive self by talking to me about our future, and that my HDC date of the 20th April isn't that far away.

During association a young Greek/English guy wants me to put him in touch with a reporter. He plans to sell a story about a catholic priest who he would supply male prostitution services to. He tells me he's inside for blackmailing the priest to the tune of £5000. The priest is from a church in the Northfield area of Birmingham. He then produces a letter from his solicitor confirming all he's just told me. It is a fascinating story which he is more than happy to share with me. Our conversation is interrupted by another inmate who wants me to write a letter for him to the judge in his case. He's already written a letter describing his background, and what led him to commit the crime he was imprisoned for, but he asks me to use 'big words' as he puts it. I am happy to help, and begin to read what he's already written. It is a heart- breaking story of how he was abused as a child by his father. How he faced violence on a daily basis while trying to protect his three younger sisters and his mother from this brute of a man. He describes how when he went into care the care workers abused him for twelve months, and how he'd contemplated suicide on numerous occasions. Of course I write his letter using 'big words', I write it as sympathetically as I can.

Our cell doors are locked at 7.30pm. I spend the evening watching TV, including Question Time with BNP boss Nick Griffin, who takes an inevitable battering. Lights out 1.30am.

Friday 23rd Oct

Wake at 7.24am. Immediately I am in a foul mood. I've had a dream that Jess has met someone. Obviously the issue is playing on my mind as much as I'm trying not to let it. I decide to join the list of cleaners who are attending the gym. I play a couple of rounds of badminton which does the job of cheering me up a little. Back on the wing in time for lunch at 11.30am. A small sausage, half a spoon of spaghetti hoops and a baked potato, I do manage to get two apples for dessert. After lunch I work in the kit room folding towels and cleaning up. I speak to Jess at 2.30pm, great to hear her voice but she's really pissed off and very upset. We desperately try to keep the conversation upbeat but it's difficult, barely two months

131

in and Jess is really feeling the strain, hardly surprising. I tell her that we have a great future to look forward to, that we're owed some good luck and that things are going to be very different when we're back together. I need her to be strong.

In a cloud of depression I continue with the day, watch TV to take my mind off things. Jonathan Ross is interviewing Boy George who spoke of his time in prison recently. I listen intently as he describes his experience, and I compare how similar it is to what I'm going through. It helps to put my situation into perspective. Lights out 11.45pm.

Saturday 24th Oct

Up at 8.30 straight to work in the kit room until lunch time. Something resembling a beef burger, potatoes with the skins on and beans, the usual cold serving. 1.45pm attend the culmination of Black History Week. This time the venue is the sports hall. Various speakers from church groups preaching God's word and singing to a small keyboard played by an old black guy. The event brings the much needed break from the routine of prison life and I am more than happy to sing along and clap my hands to the enthusiastic beat of church gospel singing.

A buffet of soul food is laid on, the menu includes rice and peas, dumplings and jerk chicken, real authentic dishes from the Caribbean. The food is delicious and more than makes up for weeks of the prison slop we've been fed. It is the first decent meal I have had in two months and I gorge until I am close to bursting. The atmosphere is great, almost party like. Sheets have been spread out on the sport hall floor where we sit and eat our feast. Prison officers sit and eat with us, Mrs. Walker joins our small group and we chat. For this period in the sports hall I almost forget I am in prison.

I am approached by an elderly black guy who is the violinist in the band. He expresses his sadness at my situation and he begins to cry. I try to reassure him that I am okay and am hoping to be out soon, he continues to cry, struggling to tell me how much he and his wife and family love me. Though I have never met this man, or his family before, I can feel a lump the size of a melon growing in my throat. I battle to keep control and just when I think I have, another elderly gent from the group approaches. As he stares at me he asks me to confirm that I am Ashley Blake, which I do. He then expresses his opinions in much the same way as the previous chap did. Then, behind his glasses, tears begin to roll down his cheeks. He keeps hugging me and squeezing my hand expressing his love. His affection catches me off guard, but I return the tactile gesture and embrace him back. Although he is a complete stranger to me, and this is a strange situation, this is the only affection I have received in two months. I battle to hold back my tears as he walks away to compose himself. When he returns a few minutes later he tells me that he didn't expect his day to turn out like this, and although he isn't happy to see me in here, he is happy to have met me, and that he is now able to report back to his wife that I am okay. A tear does leave my eye when I get back to my cell, in fact quite a few tears.

Sunday 25th Oct

Awake early today, 7.15am. The clocks have gone back but the body clock hasn't. I am expecting it to be very quiet today, but I work hard in the kit room having taken a delivery of fresh kit from the laundry department.

I call Jess at around 11.00am, she is still in bed enjoying a well-earned lie in. The afternoon is spent reading the papers and watching TV, lights out 10.30pm.

Monday 26th Oct

7.20am, body clock still adjusting. 8.30 door unlocked, I go straight to work. I am in a strange mood today, feeling very down and bored. As the day goes on every minute seems to get longer, a real drag.

11.30am lunch time. As we are being unlocked to collect our usual cold offering from the servery, I hear a commotion involving a female officer. I can't see anything as with the echo of the wing it is hard to establish exactly where the screams are coming from. The alarm bells ring, and dozens of officers from around the prison are on the wing within seconds. Turns out an inmate had taken a dislike to Miss Ellis over a disagreement and a fight ensued. He was dragged to the floor and restrained by no less than eight male officers, a technique known as "being twisted up" by inmates. He is carried off to the block.

After lunch, while I help my colleagues with their duties, the wing echoes with my name *"BLAKE!"*, which officer Kane shouts at the top of his voice from the upper landing. No need I think, as even the slightest whisper can be heard from one end of the wing to the other, but this is a man who likes his uniform, I mean *really* likes his uniform. As I answer his call by walking towards him, I remind myself that while I'm in here, this man can make my life a misery and before I reach him I conclude that this is the last thing I need. I'll have to win him around in some other way. The reason for his bellowing my name? So he can show me how to flatten cardboard boxes in order to get more into the bins!

Spend much of this afternoon keeping myself to myself in my cell, and although my door is unlocked I am not interrupted.

I speak to Jess on the phone around 6.30, she sounds upbeat and her enthusiasm rubs off on me, I will be seeing her tomorrow when she visits and we're both looking forward to it.

7.30pm and I settle down to watch the first in a new series of *Inside Out*, the BBC One primetime programme I had fronted for more than seven years. The top story is about bullying in the NHS, this is a story I produced earlier this year after I had been taken off screen. The story is linked to the restaurant that I owned in that I was having a conversation with a customer, Louise Stokes, during which I learned that she was a former nurse who had been forced to leave the NHS because she had been a victim of bullying. To cut a long story short, after several meetings I persuaded Louise to blow the whistle and we would make a programme about it for *Inside Out*. And there it was, our work on the telly with me watching it whilst sat in a prison cell. I feel proud but also an extreme sense of disappointment. Another reminder of how quickly life can change.

Tuesday 27th Oct

My body clock is struggling to adjust to the hour change and I wake at 7.00am. I am on the list to attend the gym, I'm also excited as Jess is visiting today, and the canteen with all the treats I've ordered is due to be delivered this afternoon, so I'm looking forward to what should be a good day.

As I queue for the gym Officer Clark tells me that I can't go as I am on the transfer list to Stafford. Shocked, I begin to say my goodbyes to my new colleagues, Streeter, Kristian, Anthony, Gilly and so on. I thank them for looking after me and for making my stay as good as they possibly could. I return to my cell and begin to pack my belongings. As word gets around the wing that I am off, I am soon joined by several of my colleagues headed by Matto. They don't want me to leave and advise me to see the Senior Officer, Mr. Aspberry. I agree and we all file down to the main office and ask to speak to Mr. Aspberry. He listens to our pleas and responds by saying there is nothing he can do. With that I return to my cell to continue packing. More visitors arrive to say their goodbyes, some with farewell gifts of *burn*, (prison-speak for tobacco). Raj is sad to see me go and asks me to write to him. They all advise me to be myself at my new place, and assure me that I'll be okay. Even officer Skitt shakes my hand and tells me that it was good to meet me. I hate goodbyes at the best of times, and these guys aren't making it easy for me. I'm already an emotional wreck and leaving the relative comfort and security of my new colleagues and my learned regime of Winson Green's N Wing to go to somewhere completely alien to me on my own is daunting to say the least. I have just enough time to phone Jess to let her know that I am on the move, and that's when it really hits me. I was looking forward so much to seeing her today and now I won't be able to, she is equally upset and immediately begins to research Stafford Prison on the internet.

I am taken to reception where I change into the clothes I'd arrived in. My brown suit, white shirt and black shoes. I had thought that the next time I'd be wearing these I would also be wearing a huge smile as I'd be going home to Jess, however, this is not to be. I am handcuffed to an officer to walk three steps into the waiting prison van. Through the main entrance I catch my first view in two months of the outside world. It is strange to see people walking, drivers driving, going about their daily business, oblivious to the hell I am going through in the back of this van journeying to my next fate, whatever that will be.

The first stop is at Featherstone prison, the north side of the city of Wolverhampton. The first time I'd seen this place was almost a year ago to the day. I was presenting a DVD for Staffordshire Police about the justice system, I feel nothing but irony. Two prisoners are off-loaded, and within twenty minutes we are on our way again. As I arrive at HMP Stafford it is like starting my sentence all over again, the journey, the reception committee, the piles of paperwork. During this time the officer allows me to make a two minute phone call to let Jess know where I am, and the details she needs when booking to visit. I struggle to get all the required information into my two minute slot. There is time for Jess to give me some words of support and a bit of history about Stafford prison she's learned through her research. Her words work at keeping me strong.

HMP Stafford

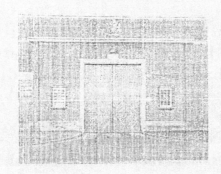

WELCOME TO
HMP
STAFFORD

INDUCTION
AND
INFORMATION
BOOKLET

SO G Vuckolc
SO Hulme

UPDATED April 2009

1

I make the officers aware that I may be a target and that I am vulnerable to attack, something I was advised to do at Winson Green. One of the officers understands my concerns and puts me in a cell on my own. I am told that there are no single cells available but the chap that usually occupies cell C3-16 is in the block for a week so I can go in there until I'm settled. I take my belongings and enter a dingy, dark and very dirty cell. The door is immediately slammed and locked behind me.

Word soon gets around of my arrival and once again I become the centre of attention. Although locked behind the cell door, the flap is constantly opened, and the small rectangular window is crammed full of curious faces peering through to confirm the rumour. I feel like I am the latest exhibit at a zoo.

My new accommodation is slightly bigger than the last but it's very old and filthy. Lime-green coloured walls, a creaky double bunk, sagging through decades of use, and a window high up near to the ceiling offering no view whatsoever. There's a door through to a separate toilet and wash basin.

5.45pm and my door is unlocked for dinner. Fish in breadcrumbs, mashed potato, and white cabbage. It looks and tastes much better than at Winson Green, and the temperature is just right. Despite the tasty food I would much rather be back at Winson Green in N4-19. I'm very close to tears once again. I don't think I'm going to get on here as well as I did in The Green, I can feel it. What a day, started off so positive and now I've reached the other end of the scale, an emotional roller-coaster. Lights out 10.15pm.

Wednesday 28th Oct. Day 56, 8 weeks

Wake up at 7.30am after an incredibly bad night's sleep. My cell door is unlocked at 8.30. Am taken to an induction meeting which consists of a two minute talk by a very young Asian women Psychologist who is clearly very nervous. As she speaks she keeps constant eye contact with me rather than referring to the whole group of ten others. I am taken back to the cell which gives me the opportunity to clean it. I am able to acquire some much sought after cleaning products from one of the wing cleaners Taff. He's a Hells Angel who I'd reported on following the murder of his

145

friend Gerry Tobin. He was gunned down while riding his motorcycle along the M40 after the Bulldog Bash in 2008. Taff is very friendly, and tells me if there is anything I need I was just to ask. He gives me cloths, a mirror, soap and a tube of toothpaste from his cell, which more resembles a small hardware store. How he managed to acquire such an array of products is beyond me, but I am grateful and set about scrubbing my new abode.

Feeling extremely low today. Tried desperately to snap myself out of it, but failed on every attempt. I decide I'm going to ask my solicitor to try to get me out of here to a category D prison.

11.45, the quiet wing erupts into a hive of activity as inmates return from their morning work or education, for lunch. Two sausages, a baked potato, spaghetti hoops served hot, and a biscuit for dessert.

I am desperate to phone Jess, but unlike at Winson Green I am unable to use the phone whenever my door is unlocked, here I do not have that privilege yet.

During the afternoon I am given the chance to visit the prison library, I also complete another application for Cat D hoping for better luck this time. I receive a letter from Jess which she only posted last night, it is great to hear from her.

I just don't feel comfortable here, is it because I'm the newcomer? I don't think so, I just have a really bad feeling in the pit of my stomach about this place, for the first time while inside I feel scared. I am fully enrolled into a boarding school of criminality.

6.15, the doors are unlocked for association giving me my first chance of the day to phone Jess. It's great to talk to her and I try to sound as though I'm fine, but she detects in my voice that I'm not. We decide she will speak to my solicitor as soon as she can to sort out my appeal and to try to get me transferred from here. Jess becomes very worried and I try to reassure her that I'll be okay, but she feels helpless. We say our goodbyes as the queue for the phone is increasing. I take a shower after which a young mixed race guy introduces himself to me. Leon Williams is from the Wyerley Birch estate which is not far from my restaurant. We chat and he invites me into a game of dominos with a small group of black men. They are very welcoming, and the noisiest game of dominos follows. 8.00pm and it's time for bang up. After the game and speaking to Jess I feel slightly better.

Thursday 29th Oct.

I awake at 8.00am and am invited to exercise, which is walking clockwise around a forty by forty foot yard, enclosed by a twenty foot high mesh fence topped with the all too familiar razor wire. Allotted time; thirty minutes.

Back on the wing I am asked to move cells, I am told to move to the 2's landing, to cell number C2-06. In there is a chap by the name of Dave Young-Smith who I immediately recognize as being one of my cleaning colleagues back at Winson Green. The reason I am given for my move is that this is a much quieter part of the wing where I won't receive as much attention from other inmates. It also houses around ten inmates, all part of the wing cleaning team, much the same as I've been used to at my previous prison. In the process of moving I am interrupted by a young lady from the prison's Psychology department. She takes me into a small meeting room where we discuss my worries and needs. I explain that I feel vulnerable due to my being recognized as the bloke off the telly. I explain that whilst working on programmes such as *Inside Out* and *Watchdog* I was responsible for exposing some very dodgy characters, I am worried that it may only be a matter of time before I come face to face with one of them, and that is a cause for concern for my safety. I also explain that by sharing a cell, my cell mate has easy access to my personal letters and could sell them to the press. She understands all of my concerns and says she'll write a report. Within the next two hours I am called into the main office by the senior officer, Miss Gaughan. Miss Gaughan is an extremely nice lady with over twenty years' experience as a prison officer, she assures me that I'll be okay if I give it time, in other words she can't or won't be moving me to a single cell just yet. My aim is to go to G Wing which is a 'super enhanced' wing, all single cells with their own separate shower and toilet. To get there you need to be suitable and recommended by your senior officer. I'm told it is too soon for me to be recommended.

This evening my new cell mate Dave and I get to know each other a bit better. We spend much of the evening chatting. Dave is forty-six, tattooed from head to toe, he looks like a right bruiser, someone who you certainly wouldn't want to meet in an alleyway late at night. Turns out he's a really nice bloke though. He tells me about his eight kids from two partners and he goes through all their personalities while showing me photos he's stuck on the walls and cupboards of our cell. He has a history of jail starting with detention centres when he was just fourteen years old followed by a fifteen year stretch in a man's jail. Today he's a hard working builder with his own Company, he also has shares in a pub in Burton Upon Trent. This time he has been sentenced to two years for arson, a dispute with neighbours which went horribly wrong. We get on well and it's pleasant to at least have someone to talk to instead of just watching telly. I get my head down at around midnight, Dave kindly turns the volume down on the TV but decides he will continue to watch a film until 3.00am. The volume and light from the TV means I can't sleep. Dave turns the telly off shortly after 3am, and I am relieved when the cell is plunged into a quiet darkness. The peace is shattered with what I first think is someone using a pneumatic drill to attempt an escape, it is Dave, he's begun to snore, the noise is so loud and annoying I don't get a wink of sleep all night.

Friday 30th Oct.

Dave wakes at around 8am, I am close to tears with anger and frustration brought on by not having received any shut eye the entire night. I explain to Dave in the best possible way that he's kept me awake all night and he responds by telling me that he is aware of his problem, and his previous cell mate had to move because of it. As soon as the cell door is unlocked I go to the office to speak to Miss Gaughan, the wing's senior officer. Her response to my complaint is that I am in the best place here at the moment, and I'll have to get used to the snoring. She offers alternative cell mates who, she advises me, could be worse than the one I have. I accept her advice to get some earplugs from the nurse and to persevere.

The nice lady from psychology has come to see me again. She's been considering my situation and wants to report three options to me;

1. I can be moved to the VP's wing. Vulnerable Prisoners are housed in a completely separate part of the prison. The type of inmate varies from former police officers, prison officers to paedophiles, rapists and other sex offenders.
2. Section 44 of the Prison Orders. This is for Vulnerable Prisoners who are constantly protected from everyone else. It's complete isolation.
3. G wing. This is the super enhanced wing of the prison with the luxury of your own cell complete with en-suite and remote control for the TV.

This option is ideal I think, however, this wing only houses forty prisoners and there are no vacancies. I will be recommended, but I'll have to wait. The nice lady leaves saying she will write a report.

Later, I am summoned to the office by senior officer Miss Gaughan. She's received the report from the nice lady from

Psychology and reiterates what she said earlier, there is nothing that can be done at the moment. We agree that I will at least give it until next Thursday to adjust. To help me settle in I am given an unpaid job assisting the wing cleaners with their duties. Rather than a specific role I just muck in with whatever needs doing, from mopping floors to sorting clothes in the kit room, and helping on the food servery. This gives me the opportunity to meet the other guys and to learn how things work at my new prison. Another set of new colleagues who are all very helpful and welcoming to me.

Today I am able to order a quilt and feather pillows from the catalogue. A luxury I seize upon with great excitement. No more make shift hard pillows, a proper feather pillow just like at home is sure to aid a restful night's sleep.

With my new role I am able to use the phone pretty much whenever I want again, so I phone Jess to reassure her that despite my predicament I am actually doing okay, and she is not to worry about me.

5.30, and it is time to serve dinner. I am given the job of handing out "brew packs". These are small, see-through, plastic bags containing four tea bags, four sachets of sugar and four of whitener. Whilst handing these out I feel extremely exposed. My role gives all the inmates on my wing the chance to see me face to face. I am very much the topic of conversation in the queue, and am the subject of much pointing, looking and whispering. Out of one-hundred-and-twenty hungry inmates only one makes a sarcastic comment about how I'd managed to gain a job so soon after arriving, a tall young lad I hear taking the piss while in the queue. When he reaches me he snatches the brew pack from my hand and says

"How come you got a job so quick?" to which I respond

"I'm just helping out."

"Yeah, but so soon, it must be favouritism!" he replies,

"No it's called being polite" I say.
He then responds with an aggressive stare and barks at me

"You saying I'm not polite?"

His loudness is for effect and he gets the attention he seeks as everyone left in the queue pauses and waits to see what is going to happen next. Luckily officers are all around and tell the young lad to move on. He does so, mumbling words I can't work out. My heart misses a couple of beats during this incident as I thought for no reason I'm going to end up with his dinner all over me, thankfully I haven't, but this is the kind of vulnerability I am worried about.

After dinner Dave and I decide to bang-up at around 6.30pm. We chat, a good conversation about all sorts for the rest of the evening. I get my head down at around 11.45pm, Dave continues to watch TV. I insert my newly acquired earplugs which help cut out the volume from the telly and later, fifty percent of Dave's snoring. At least it is an improvement on the night before and I manage some sleep.

Saturday 31st Oct.

Wake up at 8.00am to the smell of a cooked breakfast. Sausage, tomato, fried egg, all served piping hot, what a treat.

I speak to Jess at 11.30, she's spoken to my solicitor who has faxed a letter of concern to the prison governor. After lunch I am summoned to the office once again by senior officer Miss Gaughan, who suggests I write down the names of all the people I've exposed during the course of my television work. If they were to end up at HMP Stafford then they'd know to keep them away from me. This is a ridiculous idea, how am I supposed to remember the names of all those people during ten years in investigative journalism?

Sunday 1st Nov.

Wake at around 8.20am after another night listening to Dave's snoring. Wearing the earplugs is better but the sound is that loud that the most annoying noise in the world can still be heard. Soon after the cell door is unlocked I receive a visit from a prison officer who shall remain nameless. The reason for this is that it is an unofficial visit. The officer is a friend of a friend on the outside. They give me reassurances that I am in the right place as far as prisons go, and that my welfare is being looked after while I am resident. This message works in that I feel much better as to where I am, and that if I wait patiently I will settle here for the duration of my sentence.

The cell door remains unlocked for much of the day enabling Dave and I to mill around with our colleagues and waste time. Sunday lunch is served at 1.30pm, roast chicken, sprouts, potatoes and cabbage, followed by treacle pudding and smooth custard for dessert, all served hot which is still a novelty for me. I continue to carry out my unofficial job of ladling the custard into one-hundred-and-twenty dessert bowls during service, allowing my fellow inmates to get used to seeing me around so I will cease to be treated like an exciting new exhibit.

The rest of this afternoon is spent reading my third book since being inside until dinner is served. I am given the job of handing out the breakfast cereals for the next day.

Soon after dinner I am summoned to the Head of Residence's office, it is like being taken to the Headmasters office. I am escorted along the wing by Miss Gaughan who tells me it is something to do with a fax that has been sent by my solicitor. Arriving at the office I am told to wait outside while Miss Gaughan knocks on the door and goes in. I wait like a delinquent school child, and after a few minutes I am called in. I walk through the doorway into what even looks like my old headmasters office. I glance around and see a large man sat behind a suitably large desk, there are soft, sofa-like chairs facing him. I assume the stance of a naughty school-boy standing in front with a worried look on my face. I am politely asked to take a seat. He begins by referring to the letter my solicitor has faxed to the prison. Then, to allay my fears, he tries to convince me that it is highly unlikely that I'll be the recipient of any revenge attack from anyone I've exposed whilst I was working on *Watchdog*, which he refers to as *Crimewatch*. I respond by telling him as long as I'm accessible I'm concerned for my safety, and that it is only a matter of time before someone has a go. I am told that my concerns are being taken seriously. Then the subject changes to concerns about my visitors. Mr. Haynes is concerned that most of the people who are coming to visit me are likely to be friends who are also journalists, he reminds me that the rules say they can visit, but they're not allowed to report anything that they see, or we discuss. I agree that I understand. After all the official business is dealt with Mr. Haynes tells me that he was a regular visitor to my restaurant and rated the Thai food. He also enquires as to whether I am still a keen motorcyclist. We chat informally for a few minutes before I leave the office hoping to have impressed him enough to speed up my transfer to G-Wing.

Back in my cell Dave and I chat until about 1.00am, I get my head down leaving Dave to watch the TV.

Monday 2nd Nov (two months)

I managed to get some sleep last night but the quality was dreadful due to Dave's snoring. It's beginning to show on my face, puffy eyes, I'm knackered. My sentence has effectively doubled. Not only am I awake during the day but throughout the night too, it's like I'm being tortured. Here's how it works: Dave watches TV until the wee small hours and although he turns the volume down I can still hear it, and the light illuminates the small cell. When he eventually switches the TV off, he begins to snore within minutes of falling asleep. It's so loud even our next door neighbours can hear him through the reinforced thick stone walls. I was forced from what little sleep I could snatch at 6.45am. I made a coffee not caring how much noise I made, this was revenge, but it didn't work, although Dave stirred he didn't wake up, my pathetic attempts to interrupt his shut-eye failed, he was dead to the world.

As I write this diary entry the BBC News at 1.00pm has just started, Dave is snoring, he's napping after having just eaten lunch. How dare he! Perhaps if he didn't sleep during the day then he'd be able to sleep earlier at night and not keep me awake with telly watching. Mind you that would mean I'd have to endure many more hours listening to his torturous noise, I can't win. So angry!

This afternoon, part of my induction is spent carrying out a literacy and numeracy test, the same as I completed at Winson Green. I am informed about various courses and jobs that are available within the prison.

Tuesday 3rd Nov

Another sleepless night. Bleary eyed get straight to work mopping a small shower cubicle and generally helping out where I can. 10.00am I hear the nurse is on the wing so I decide to pay a visit to enquire about Hepatitis injections, something I've been advised to do during my arrival at HMP Stafford on the 27th October. I wait outside a small gated room with four other inmates. The gate is unlocked by a tall bearded man called Ben who asks for the next person to enter. I am offered this place by the other inmates. I enter the small room where I immediately see the nurse who advised me to see her about the injections whenever she is on the wing. The nurse, called Sam, tells me she is dealing with doctor's appointments today, and can I see her another time. I agree and leave, the whole conversation lasts no more than ten seconds. I return to help out with cleaning duties.

Jess is paying a visit today, the first for a few weeks and I'm excited to see her.

Lunch is served at 11.45 and Dave and I return to our cell to eat while the doors are locked. Shortly after being locked the cell door is opened by Officer Preece who hands me a piece of paper. I ask what it is, he tells me it is an *underachieved*.

"What for?" I ask politely,

"Something to do with the nurse." he tells me.

Surprised and confused I begin to delve deeper as to why I've been given an *underachieved*. Officer Preece can't help, and tells me if I receive any more *underachieveds* I will be dropped from Enhanced status to Basic, losing all the privileges I've gained so far.

An *underachieved* is a black mark against an inmate who misbehaves in anyway. A report is kept on your prison file. Receive three and your privileges are stopped and whatever status you've reached gets dropped back, thus Enhanced to Standard, Standard to Basic, below Basic then you spend time in The Block, solitary confinement, for however long the Senior Officer deems punishment is necessary. No

TV, no visits, no canteen. It's not somewhere I want to be.

Officer Preece locks the cell door leaving me to scan the form in detail.

Prisoner's name:	BLAKE	Prisoner's n°:	GN7762	Location:	C26
Session:	AM / PM	Work area:	B|C treatment room		
Day:	Tuesday	Date:	3|11|09		

* delete as applicable

✓ relevant box

☐ Overachieved

☑ Underachieved

Comments to support decision:

claimed he needed to see de - walked into treatment room - did not have appointment was told to get out and follow normal procedure

Signed: .... Date: 3/11/09.

Member of staff

Print name: .... HAhEmayer ....

IEP AWARD RECORD

The above reads: *Claimed he needed to see Dr. - walked into treatment room - Did not have appointment, was told to get out and follow normal procedure.*

This inevitably puts a downer on my mood, I am angry but also very worried. I want to progress through my sentence as trouble-free as possible, and I don't want anything to stand in my way of my move to G Wing, or my chance of the earliest release possible.

1.40pm and I'm taken to the visits block. It is great to see Jess, although she can tell something is wrong. I don't tell her about my *underachieved*, I don't want to worry her. Jess does a great job of cheering me up with talk of our future together once this blip, as she calls it, is over. We talk of getting married and having a baby, Jess wants a girl, she can have whatever she wants, she deserves it, she's my soul-mate. The visit is over all too soon and I am back on the wing.

I have the chance to speak to Officer Barker about my *underachieved*, he advises me not to worry about it and to speak to the person whose written it. Mr. Barker is very understanding of my concerns and believes it to be a simple misunderstanding. Word soon gets around about my *underachieved*, and my new colleagues take the piss for much of the afternoon as you'd expect.

Dave and I don't watch a single programme on the TV all evening, instead we recount stories of our past, which become very deep at times. Dave tells me about the death of his Mum, then his Dad, then his sister, he tells me of the time when he stabbed the person who'd abused his sister and the time when he came face to face with the man who killed his mother in a car crash. It is the first time he's spoken to anyone about it and apologizes for crying, I think it has done Dave the world of good to let it out to me. Having learned more about one another we turn out the light at midnight. But it is another sleepless night for both of us. Dave can't sleep, he's opened a cavern of emotions which are playing on his mind.

Weds 4th Nov.

The cell door is unlocked at 8.20am. I am keen to rectify this misunderstanding regarding my *underachieved*. It has been playing on my mind all night, it has affected my mood, and it worried Jess during her visit yesterday. I need to sort this out as soon as I possibly can, so I go to the nurses room to see the author of the complaint Ben. He isn't there, however, Sam the nurse is and so I explain what has happened and she too agrees that it must be a misunderstanding, and she'll have a word the next time she sees Ben.

The rest of the day is spent reading a book chatting with my cleaning colleagues and generally wasting time, once our cleaning duties are done there isn't anything left to do, it's a matter of wasting as much time as you can. A chap called Dave from Coventry stops by my cell to say hello and expresses his disgust at the way I've been treated by the judge. He tells me that he and his Mum were fans and enjoyed watching the news whenever I was on. The interesting thing about Dave is he purports himself as a bit backward, a bit dim but I find he's actually the opposite. He relies on this impression to get him through his sentence and get on with everyone even if he is often the butt of jokes, his humour endears him to most inmates, very clever I think. Dave is in for cutting the brake cables on his lover's husband's car, he got caught having got stuck under the car due to being overweight. He also confessed to arson and substance abuse and recounts the story of when he was sniffing lighter fuel while drying his clothes on a clothes horse in front of a three bar electric fire. He was sniffing that much lighter fuel that the front

166

room of his gran's house exploded into a fire ball burning his rack of clothes, himself, and charring the entire room. Dave's stories provide me with the much needed humour I have been lacking, and it is great to meet him.

During the afternoon while the wing is quiet I take a shower in a sort of private single shower room we have the privilege of using on our part of the wing. Whilst in full lather four of my new colleagues burst in wearing rubber gloves and tell me it is time for my initiation. Thankfully they were joking, but it does mean I've been accepted into this group.

I speak to Jess at around 6.30pm, as usual it is great to hear her voice. I apologize for being miserable during her visit, and tell her how much I love her.

Back in my cell at 7.00pm where a short letter from my best pal Gez is waiting. I've spoken to him only once since being inside. I purposely haven't spoken to him as it would evoke great memories of what two best mates get up to when they're out and about. We've been through a lot together and have always looked out for each other, but on this occasion there's nothing he can do and I'm sure he understands my lack of contact.

Thursday 5th Nov.

Another sleepless night, Dave's snoring seems to be getting worse. I get up at 8.15am I'm knackered. Straight to work scrubbing the communal showers which haven't seen a scrubbing brush or detergent for what must be decades. They are sparkling after two hours, a job well done. Then it is on to rubbish and recycling drop off. On the way back I notice Ben is in attendance at the nurses' room so I stop by to try to sort out the *underachieved* he'd issued to me. I show him a copy of the complaint he'd written and I suggest it is a simple misunderstanding and could he retract it. I am joined by Dayley Hall, a fellow inmate, who witnessed my first visit and short conversation with the nurse about Hep. B injections, he helps remind Ben about what actually happened. Ben responds by saying he won't retract the *underachieved*, and if we persist he will write another one. Surprised at his response I inform him that he has left me no alternative but to make a formal complaint, to which he responds "Do what you like!" With that Dayley and I leave.

Back in my cell I am fuming at Ben's attitude, and set about writing a formal complaint whilst Dayley is out on the wing telling as many people that will listen about what has just happened. My complaint writing is interrupted by a visit from Russ, nicknamed 'Rent-a-Gob' for his loud, sometimes overbearing and hugely exaggerated story telling. He's heard about my troubles with Ben and has come to offer his advice. He says I should just forget about it, and that I shouldn't go up against the system. He reckons I have it cushy here and shouldn't upset that by making a complaint. I consider what he's said, but the journalist inside me has to right this wrong. If that leads to me being treated badly by the system then so be it, this man should not be allowed to get away with this abuse of power, I never could stand bullies. After completing my complaint I post it in the box for the Governor.

That evening is spent with Dave and I chatting, and occasionally with our faces pressed against the small window trying to catch a glimpse of the fireworks lighting up Bonfire Night over Stafford town centre.

Friday 6th Nov.

It's quite busy for the wing cleaners on Fridays, as well as the usual cleaning duties we have to co-ordinate a kit change for the entire wing. This means swapping dirty clothes and bed-wear for clean ones. The canteen is also delivered so the mood is generally upbeat. During this I overhear my colleagues debating how much they'd get paid by the newspapers for snapping a picture of me in prison. They are discussing the best picture options: lying on my bunk, eating off a plastic plate, me in the shower, and so they go on. They settle on getting a picture of me with rubber gloves on mopping the showers, their next task is to find someone with a camera phone.

I receive the results of my Mandatory Drugs Test this afternoon which, of course comes back negative.

HMP
STAFFORD

MANDATORY DRUG TEST
RESULT

NO. CN2262 NAME Blake

LOCATION C2-06

YOUR TEST TAKEN ON 27/10/09 (DATE)
HAS PROVED NEGATIVE.

SIGNED D Wlise

171

Sat 7th Nov.

Wake to the smell of cooked breakfast. Sausages, fried egg, tomato. Cooked breakfasts are served here at weekends unlike at Winson Green.

Dave has become far too comfortable with me in the cell, as well as his tortuous snoring he's began to fart. Loud and forceful. Sharing this small space is becoming unbearable and I make it known that it's not a very nice thing to be doing in such a confined place. He responds by laughing.

I speak to Jess at 10.30am, it's great to hear her, but she has bad news which she's scared to tell me for fear it will tip me over the edge. She's had word from my solicitor who told her my Appeal has failed. Jess has been up much of the night worrying about how she would break this bombshell - but it doesn't come as a huge shock to me, a huge disappointment yes, but with the way my luck has gone lately I hadn't placed much hope on a positive outcome with the appeal. Jess is relieved by my reaction, I can hear her voice lighten once she's assessed my response.

This afternoon is spent banged up watching TV while Dave sleeps, snores and farts, helped by the chilli con carne he had chosen for his lunch.

I'm smoking much more and I haven't been to the gym since Winson Green.

Monday 9th Nov.

8.30 I'm told to report to the Education Department where I am booked onto a Resettlement Course. The tutor doesn't turn up so we are asked to complete some paperwork. Questions on the form ask me to list any qualifications and work history. Whilst answering it brings home to me what a desperate situation I am in, but nevertheless, I decide to persevere and give this course a chance. You never know, I may just learn something, and in any event, it will look good on my prison file when it comes to deciding early release. Having completed the paperwork the group of eight sits debating how bad Stafford prison is. This is news to me as I only have Winson Green to compare Stafford to, however, the rest of the group have the knowledge of various prisons round the country, and each votes that Stafford is by far the worst. The

consensus does cause me concern, have I
ended up in the worst prison?

After lunch it is back to the same classroom
for much of the same as the morning
session. The course will teach the very
basics of human life, from how to boil an
egg to how to manage money.

Tuesday 10th Nov.

Spent much of last night shouting at Dave
to stop snoring. Attend class at 8.45am to
be taught how to write a cheque and to
discuss what income and expenditure is.
Now, I don't consider myself to be a know it
all, far from it but I do feel a certain amount
of guilt as surely I am taking the place on
this course that would be better occupied by
someone who needs it. At 11.00am the
monotony of the classroom session is broken
when an officer enters and announces
"anyone for the library". At least I can now
get a book and perhaps learn something.

Lunch today is two sausages, boiled
potatoes, a hot dog bun and curry sauce, at
least it is hot. On the way to my cell Miss
Gaughan informs me that my official
complaint about Ben has been dealt with,

and I am relieved when she tells me it has been removed from my file. It was decided that it was a misunderstanding and that will be the end of the matter.

After lunch I am told to attend the gym for an induction. A talk on health and safety and then some more filling out of paperwork after which we are allowed to use the gym facilities. After being given a pair of prison issue shorts, a vest and some plimsolls I play a few games of badminton followed by soft tennis. I appreciate the chance to do something active, to break out into a sweat.

Weds 11th Nov.

My cell mate Dave and I had put our names on the list to attend a chapel memorial service to pay our respects to the fallen on Armistice Day. When we arrive it soon becomes obvious that we are the only two from the entire prison to be from a main wing. The twenty-five others are VP's, Vulnerable Prisoners, made up of paedophiles and sex offenders. Not one to generalize but they all have a similar look, their demeanour is sluggish, their appearance is scruffy, tattooed, many with

175

long shiny, greasy looking hair. They converse as though they have the guilt of conscience weighing them down. I am fascinated by them and try hard not to judge. As we drink coffee a few of them come over to chat. I feel myself reluctant to shake their hand as they offer it to me, but I do so out of politeness. Dave chooses not to shake anyone's hand as he stands close by telling them that he is my body guard.

The memorial service consists of hymn singing, poems and readings by inmates and prayers. I'm not a religious man, I am there to pay my respects to the war dead, The service means so much more to Dave, he lost his brother in Afghanistan in 2007.

After the service more coffee and small talk. Marjory, who played the organ in the chapel singles me out. Taking me to one side she asks whether I'd be interested in becoming the chapel orderly. This would involve keeping the chapel clean, organized and tidy, making tea and coffee, and greeting church goers. Sounds like the ideal prison job. I am delighted to be asked, this will mean I wouldn't have to attend the classroom anymore. I can't help feeling a small amount of excitement as we're led back to our cell in time for lunch.

This afternoon I am told to continue to attend the education department until the job of chapel orderly comes through. Whilst making my way along the corridor a lady is struggling while wheeling office style chairs from one room into another so I offer to lend a hand. She's surprised at my offer but gladly accepts. As we're moving the chairs a realization comes over her face, she pauses, and speechless she mouths to me

"Are you Ashley"?

"Yes," I reply. "Pleased to meet you."

"I'm Rose, I run the creative writing class and I could do with some help with a play I'm producing", she says.

I explain that I'm trying to get off this education course as it's not for me and that I am waiting for the chapel position to become available, but in the meantime I'd be happy to help. She tells me she'll be in touch and thanks me for helping her. This is the sixth job I've been offered since being locked up.

During the afternoon lesson we complete several very common sense tests on health and safety and food hygiene, I'm learning nothing new and I'm happy to help those who are struggling. Many in the class become disruptive forty minutes into the afternoon session. I witness half a dozen grown men behaving like four years olds at pre-school making it perfectly clear they don't want to be there. The female tutor in her early thirties is struggling to keep control and I can't help but wonder why she's chosen this as her career. Attempting to keep the class's attention she confiscates a deck of rude playing cards from two inmates who are gambling for cigarettes. No sooner does she put the cards in her draw, at the opposite end of the table another two are playing drafts. The tutor eventually persuades the class that as long as we get through todays work then we can play games. The group reluctantly agree, and the learning process begins again. It's not long before I'm reminded again of the juvenile atmosphere when an inmate asks to go to the toilet the tutor agrees and hands him a small credit card size piece of laminated card bearing the words: *Out of class Pass* and on the back it said: *The bearer of this pass has been authorised by the tutor to be out of the class, NO SMOKING.* It's a pass to visit the toilet, and for which you have to sign before paying a visit.

The classwork is completed by 3.50pm and the class is allowed, as promised, to play cards, draughts, and Pac Man on the PC's before being dismissed for the day at 4.30pm.

Liver and potatoes for dinner, quite tasty. I watch my old BBC colleagues reporting the day's news on the telly as I regularly do.

6.30pm, we're due to be unlocked for association, the wing erupts into the usual hum-drum of one hundred and twenty inmates socializing, but our door remains locked, they've forgotten about us. Dave has an appointment to make a phone call to his wife and daughter, an especially important call today as it's Armistice Day, and Dave is keen to find out how the laying of the wreath on his brothers grave has gone. With no sign of being unlocked Dave presses the emergency button in the cell usually reserved for, well, emergencies and begins to time how long it will take for an officer to arrive. After fifteen minutes our cell door is still locked, Dave is getting increasingly agitated and comments that it's a good job he's not bleeding to death. He begins to bang the door and shout through the gap to attract the attention of another inmate enjoying his association. After another ten minutes Dave is successful and an inmate attracts the attention of an officer who *kind of* apologizes for forgetting to unlock us. We share some light-hearted banter before Dave and I head for the phones. I speak to Jess, she's at work so the conversation is brief, making sure we're both okay, and express how much we're looking forward to seeing each other when she visits tomorrow.

Back in the cell I spend the evening replying to letters I've received, and Dave spends much of his time in the toilet. A separate room the size of a wardrobe which houses a stainless steel toilet without a drop down seat, very cold to sit on, a stainless steel wash basin above which is a mirror tile stuck to the wall using four blobs of prison issue toothpaste, who needs *No More Nails?* Dave eventually emerges with a new look, he's shaved his beard. I can't help but take the piss, it is obvious to me that he's become clean shaven in an attempt to look less like the blokes we'd met in the chapel earlier today, the meeting has clearly had an adverse effect on my cell buddy, nevertheless, it is a new fresher look for him.

During this evening Dave and I share lines from letters written by loved ones and we reflect on our adventurous day in the chapel, we tell stories of our lives on the outside, we share laughter and we share tears. Dave shares his thoughts with me about how he wants his life to change when he's released, he wants to use his experience to help others. I tell Dave he'd be the perfect cell mate were it not for his loud snoring and equally loud farting.

Dave reads a couple of poems he's written while in here, I ask him if I can use one in this book and he agrees so here it is:

CONVICTED

Convicted by a jury to a six by ten cell, a kettle, a telly, a push button door bell. The warders, the jailers, the jangle of keys. The ill fitted windows that help you to freeze.

The barred windows and mesh obstructing the view, screaming and shouting from prisoners with nothing to do.

Pigeons are scavenging for scraps in the yard trying to get through the place not barred.

Life seems dormant, prisoners say dead. But I see freedom for I live in my head.

Reformation in prison is a word of no use - for some of the cons seem only to abuse.

They live their lives by what they feel, thinking of prison as no big deal.

How wrong they are, can't they just see.

The rights and wrongs for liberty.

Alkies and smack heads form a queue, shaking and quaking for the medics brew.

Asians with abrasions and gangster talk, swaggering and blagging when they walk.

Rudeness and attitude they don't see.

But I'm one of a kind, for freedom is my life, my liberty.

Dave has written many more poems like this, I've advised him to publish them so if you see his book on the shelf it's well worth a read. There you go Dave, I've plugged your book, but if you become a millionaire, remember your old pad mate and throw me a few quid will you?

I get my head down around midnight, but it's the usual routine of Dave watching TV, I can't sleep, telly goes off, Dave begins to snore, I can't sleep! He continues to make my days unnecessarily long.

Thursday 12th Nov

I awake at 7.30am and take down the towel we're using as a curtain from the window flooding the cell with crisp winter sunshine. Dave is still asleep on the bottom bunk and I deliberately make noise in a childish attempt to get my own back on him for keeping me awake for much of the night.

I'm apprehensive but excited, Jess is visiting today and I'm looking forward to seeing her. I head off to the classroom at 8.45am. Today's learning subject is money management and budgeting. My fellow students are paying more attention today

183

and allowing the tutor, a middle aged chap by the name of Michael to teach. Math's isn't my best subject and we're tasked with working out percentages on various hire purchase deals. I lend a hand to others who are finding it more difficult.

11.45am I head back to the wing for lunch: fishcakes, roast spuds and mushy peas. I watch the lunch time news and ready myself for Jess's visit. I change out of my usual prison wear into a blue and white striped, short-sleeve, collared shirt, and light blue jeans to look smarter and more presentable.

I make my way with forty other inmates to the visits block. We're checked in, searched and put into a small holding room until our name is called. Visits are 2.00pm till 4.00pm, however it's 2.25pm before my name is called, giving me only an hour and half with Jess. Even so, we have a fantastic visit, we hold onto each other for ages as we fill in the gaps since we last saw each other. We agree that Jess will visit every week now that I'm settled in. The time flies by, I don't feel sad as Jess reassures me that all is well with her and it will only be a week before we see each other again.

Back in my cell I catch up with my post, I've received a card from a colleague and extremely good friend Rachel Bowering. Rachel is the series Director on the BBC *Inside Out* programme and we have worked closely together for many years. In her card she tells me about the Royal Television Society Awards which she attended last week. It's *the* night out of the year in television land. I've attended for the past eight years to pick up numerous awards for the BBC's *Midlands Today* and *Inside Out* programmes. It's a great back slapping event. Last year I was given the honor of hosting the awards and as I sit here in my cell I wonder whether I'll ever go to another one. Lights out 11.30pm.

Friday 13th Nov.

Have quite a good night's sleep in comparison, only have to shout at Dave half a dozen times.

In the classroom the subject is how to write an effective CV. We watch a couple of DVD's on interview techniques, and set about writing our CV's. I find myself once again helping others with their task.

I learn from my classmates that in their opinion HMP Stafford is run more like a category B rather than a category C prison. They give me examples by comparing it to other Cat C establishments they've experienced during their time behind bars. Examples include the cell door being unlocked for most of the time, allowed showers every day, wearing own clothes, use of the telephone whenever, the food is supposed to be better and they tell me that it is illegal for the prison to have razor wire atop the walls, but they get round this by paying a fine every year. I'm also told that the prison sniffer dogs have a budget for food of £5.00 per day whereas for a prisoner the meal budget is only £1.75 per day. All interesting opinions and when I get the opportunity I must check the facts.

11.40am we break for lunch and for the weekend (always half day on Fridays). After lunch I help with the weekly kit change.

The kit change often turns into the most stressful event of the week when one-hundred-and-twenty inmates swap their entire dirty kit for clean. In order for this to happen swiftly and orderly the clean kit is spread out in order of size in the shower room, each worker has a station for example I'm on sweat shirts. There's a shouter, Craig Matthews and as each inmate arrives with their dirty kit it's swapped like for like with Craig shouting what's required, it goes like this; I need three T shirts, two tops, one track suit, one jeans size 34, then we chuck all his requirements at him, that's the fun part. The stress comes when the queue starts to build and Craig does not like to repeat himself, we either get his order wrong, or we're not quick enough. Craig becomes extremely angry very quickly and I've seen him shout, bollock, ridicule and reduce the hardest inmates to tears.

There are, however, perks to working on the kit change, you get to pick the best and newest of the kit. Vanity still exists inside.

After kit change is complete the canteen is handed out, and this week I have treated myself to all sorts of goodies in an attempt to cheer myself up.

Despatch Receipt   12/11/2009

Route/load: SF / 000425
Order Number: E550000000000151320
Customer ID: CN7762   2 of 2
Customer Name:

BLAKE ASHLEY

Prison Name: HMP STAFFORD

Location: C2-006

Product Description	Ord	Desp	Price
Swan Slimline Filter T	1	1	0.71
Amber Leaf 25g	1	1	5.42
Amber Leaf* 12.5g	1	1	2.76
Toe Nail Clipper	1	1	0.99
Dettol Antibac Bar Soa	1	1	0.84
HS Hdwash 99p 250ml	1	1	0.99
Cad DM 49g	2	2	1.00
Wine Gums 1 170g	1	1	1.00
Fruit&Nut Mix 350g	1	1	1.49
Cofresh Bombay Mix 10	1	1	0.49
Nescafe * 100g	1	1	2.75
Coke PET 1.5ltr	2	2	2.96
HS Mlk Cho Dig 109p	1	1	1.09
ES Jaffa Cake 99p	3	3	2.97
Royal Edinburgh Shortb	2	2	1.50
Prin Sard in Oil* 120	1	1	0.91
Pri Tuna Oil	2	2	2.98
DM Peach Slices in Jui	1	1	1.05
DM Pear Halves/Juice*	2	2	1.98
HS P/apple Slices/Juic	1	1	0.59

Total Ordered: 27
Total Despatched: 27   34.47

DO NOT OPEN BAGS UNTIL YOU HAVE CHECKED
THE CONTENTS. ERRORS CANNOT BE RECTIFIED
ONCE BAGS HAVE BEEN OPENED.

This evening is spent replying to letters that have been sent by colleagues and fans of my work on the television. Lights out 1.00am.

Sat 14th Nov

Woken with the door being unlocked at 8.30, I've had the first decent night's sleep since being at Stafford. Dave's snoring wasn't so annoying last night, perhaps I'm getting used to it. I collect my cooked breakfast of sausage, fried egg and tinned tomatoes and give it to Dave, I'm not a big breakfast eater.

I receive two pieces of internal mail: one dealing with my application for the chapel orderly's job, and the other is an official reply to my complaint about unfairly being given an *underachieved*.

I get to work by pushing a laundry trolley over-laden with dirty kit to the laundry department. The journey takes around ten minutes and I'm accompanied by an officer whose job it is to unlock and lock the seven gates en route. Most of the trip is outside, the sky is totally blue, sun gloriously shining, it's one of those crisp winter mornings which puts a spring in my step.

Duties complete I still have the rest of the day to waste so Dave and I set about giving our cell a good clean. By the time we've finished we can see our faces in the floor.

11.30, time to help out on the servery, my job today is to dispense the mash potatoes, only one scoop I'm told otherwise I'm off the job! One of the perks of working on the servery is that there's almost always plenty of food left over so if you have a healthy appetite you can fill your boots, I have a sweet tooth so along with Halal Curry and rice, I help myself to an extra portion of jam sponge and custard.

During this afternoon twelve of us are taken across to the reception block to pick parcels. While we're there each of us is ordered to sit in a bizarre looking grey chair for five seconds, it's called a *BOSS* Chair, an electronic scanner, and it's job is to detect whether I have a mobile phone inserted. An interesting piece of prison technology which proved none of us were about to make a phone call from our rectums!

We are called through one by one to receive and sign for our parcels, mine is the much anticipated duvet, 13.5 tog but more importantly two duck feathered pillows - heaven. Dave receives the same, plus a *Bart Simpson* duvet cover set.

We return to our sparkling clean cell and excitedly unpack our parcels. Not before long the cell is transformed into something which more resembles a six-year olds bedroom as Dave's colourful duvet cover brightens the small space. Word soon gets round and our cell becomes the centre of attention for almost the entire wing. The inevitable piss is ripped out of us, but I can also tell there is a certain amount of envy.

The sunny skies, the clean cell, the new duvets and pillows have put Dave and I in a fine mood and the humour is good today. I speak to Jess on the phone and she can hear I am in the best mood she's heard for quite a while. Our conversation is upbeat, and I reaffirm how much I love her, she does the same for me.

Good moods do not last for long in jail, sooner or later something happens to bring you right back down and reminds you exactly where you are.

When I return to my cell Dave has received a letter telling him that his friend and business partner has died suddenly, there's nothing he can do, he can't even go to the funeral.

Sunday 15th Nov

I wake with the cell door being unlocked at 8.15am. That's a sentence I never thought I'd ever write!

Despite our new purchases of duvet and luxury feathered pillows both Dave and I have had a restless night's sleep.

At 4.00pm we receive a visit from an officer to complete a cell check. This is carried out each week to ensure inmates haven't damaged the cell in anyway or aren't using the plastic cutlery to tunnel to freedom. During our inspection the officer asks Dave to remove a dozen or so photographs he has on display on the cupboard doors. It seems like a petty request and Dave decides to argue that their position is not a cause for concern. However, this officer is not an officer to be messed with. He rarely smiles and to me seems to be treading water until his day of retirement. I wouldn't put him past the age of forty-eight, and he reminds me of the type of person to have joined the prison service in the days when it was common practice for screws to beat up inmates as part of the fun of being in charge. Only now the rules have changed and the disappointment is evident on this officer's face. I try to imagine what's going through his head as he catches sight of our luxury duvet sets!

The evening is spent watching TV. I'm touched by a documentary about Great Ormond Street Children's Hospital. A film features a little boy whose life is saved because of the fantastic work of the doctors and nurses. Had it not been for the donations made by the public this little lad would almost certainly have lost his battle for life. It's not right that this boy's life depends on donations. Why is the government wasting thousands of pounds keeping someone like me in prison, surely this money could go to hospitals like this one to save young lives. The judge could have handed me a community sentence to help raise funds for this sort of thing. I think about the tens of thousands of pounds I've raised for charity using my minor celebrity status. Surely my punishment could be better served than just laying here wasting time?

Monday 16th Nov

Off to class at 8.45am and Hilary, the official course tutor who, I learn, has returned to work after losing her mother. Hilary reminds me of my cookery teacher at school. She's sixty-one years of age slightly on the large size and very pleasant. I can't help wonder why such a lovely person has chosen to work in a place like this. Today we're cooking, my favourite pastime, and I haven't cooked a meal for almost three months. I am given ingredients of one egg, a choice of one slice of either white or brown bread, I choose brown. I decide, with limited ingredients, I'll go for scrambled egg on toast. A knob of butter, a splash of milk, which is actually coffee whitener mixed with water, salt and pepper to season, and within minutes my healthy offering is beautifully presented. Others opt for a variety of fried egg or omelette, but I am amazed to discover that the guys need to be shown how to make the simplest of dishes. We sit and eat our work while Hilary chats to the group in a getting to know you kind of way. Hilary knows who I am and tries desperately not to show any kind of emotion to having the guy she's used to watching on the evening news every day sat in front of her in prison.

During the afternoon session the subject is money management and budgeting on a very low income. All extremely basic stuff but I stick with it to show willing and help others struggling with the numbers.

I did learn something new. Prisoners are allowed to have money sent in by cheque or postal order to spend on things from the canteen list and Argos catalogue. This money goes into the prison's bank account to accrue interest. With 760 prisoners in this jail alone, how much interest is generated off prisoner's personal money and where does that money go?

4.45pm class dismissed, back to the wing for dinner, something that resembles a spaghetti bolognese, but doesn't taste like one.

During association it is time for a haircut, and with the lack of professional barbers around my usual smart short back and sides is out of the question. I ask to borrow Craig

Matthews' personal clippers and ask my neighbour to do the honours. Zero all over.

Back in my cell minus a good head of hair I've received half a dozen letters from friends, colleagues and viewers which I spend much of the evening replying to.

Tuesday 17th Nov.

The door is unlocked and flung open at 8.20am by Officer Bethall, the officer who'd carried out the cell inspection at the weekend. He tells me he wants a word and I am to report to the office on my way to class. I scramble to get myself together wondering if this could be the move to G-Wing that I've so desperately been waiting for, I'm excited. I knock on the door of the office before politely being invited in to take a seat.

"Now then" he says.

Well I immediately think I haven't done anything wrong so, yes I would love to go to G-Wing, thank you very much. He continues,

"We've received these forms, two people want to know whether you're housed here"

The prison service is not allowed to confirm to the outside world where you are without your permission. People can use the prisoner location service which generates a form for the prisoner to sign giving permission for their whereabouts to be disclosed.

I have received two such forms, one from Ian Hickman, a cameraman at the BBC who I've worked with for years. The other is from a car finance company chasing payment. I disappointedly sign the paperwork and head off to class. G-Wing? Not today.

Wed 18th Nov

Nothing happened

Thursday 19th Nov.

Awake 8.00am after another night of shouting at Dave to stop snoring, the ear plugs only serve to muffle his snoring.

The cell door is unlocked by Mr. Barker this morning who tells me I have a "special visit".

9.00am I'm taken to the visits block to meet my solicitor to hear the news about why my appeal had failed.

We argue a little about how the trial had gone and I make it quite clear that I don't think my barrister did a good enough job, clearly, otherwise I wouldn't be here! Anyway, not much point in labouring over it now, I just feel the need to get it off my chest.

When I return to the wing Craig Matthews, who's the man that somehow knows everything that is happening in the prison, tells me that he's heard that I'm about to be offered a place on G-Wing. How he gets his information is beyond me but it's usually quite accurate. This news excites me but I wonder whether he's just winding me up.

After lunch it's back to the visits block, this time to see my favourite person in the entire world, Jess. We share a great visit, but as usual it's over too soon. On the way back to the wing another inmate who I've never seen before comments that I'm on my way to G-Wing, word certainly does spread quickly round these parts, I choose to believe the information and I am excited once again.

Back on C-Wing, Dayley Hall, the chap who'd helped me a few weeks ago when witnessing my *underachieved*, is protesting at my imminent move to G-Wing claiming it is unfair as I've only been here for three weeks, I am being shown favouritism. He's threatening to make an official complaint, he's turned against me.

The senior officer Miss Gaughan telephones G-Wing to confirm my move but the news isn't good. There's no room but she tells me that I'll definitely be over there before Christmas. In the meantime I'm offered an alternative by a fellow classmate Delroy Smithen, a twenty-five- year-old black guy from Leeds, who wants to share a cell with me. He assures me that he is clean and tidy, he doesn't snore and he likes to get his head down early. It would mean a move to D-Wing. After careful consideration rather than face getting to know a new cell mate again I will stay put until G-Wing comes along. Although Dave snores we get on very well, and that's extremely important when sharing such a small space.

Friday 20th Nov.

It was possibly *the* worst night's sleep, Dave hadn't taken the nasal spray to help reduce his snoring which resulted in me shouting at him the entire night. Bleary eyed I make my way to the classroom. I am barely awake to concentrate on whatever it is we are supposed to be doing.

10.45am the class is interrupted by senior officer Miss Gaughan asking for Delroy Smithen and I. We are taken out of the classroom like naughty little boys. Miss Gaughan tells us that it is our lucky day, two single cells have become available on D-Wing and we can have them.

Back to C-Wing to pack my stuff, Dave is visibly upset at my departure, he is concerned who he'll be getting as a new cell mate. For the past three weeks we have shared deep conversations, we've had a good laugh and we've found that despite completely different backgrounds we have a lot in common. I shall miss him, but not his snoring and farting.

D-Wing

My arrival at D-Wing is the usual welcome response of inmates staring, pointing, and whispering. I'm given cell number D1-19. It's down at basement level. The cell is freezing, tiny and narrow, four foot by twelve foot, it has a separate toilet. It's filthy. There's a TV but no kettle. As I get to work cleaning my new home a tall, good looking mixed race guy arrives at my door, he introduces himself as Elliot, he welcomes me to D-Wing and tells me to come to him if there's anything I need. He sees the state of my cell and offers me a broom, mop and bucket, and some cleaning detergent from his own personal stash. He is the Number One on the wing and I am privileged to have been personally welcomed by him, let alone have the use of his personal cleaning equipment.

It isn't long before I have the cell spick-n-span as my dear Mum would say. An officer arrives with a brand new kettle, Mr. Robinson becomes my new personal officer, and shortly after lunch Officer Reeves arrives with a key to my cell, the first key I have held in almost three months. Although the cell was cold and tiny, I shall miss Dave and my colleagues on C-Wing. I'm looking forward to a good, early night's sleep without having to listen to Dave's snoring.

The evening is spent watching BBC *Children In Need*. I have hosted *Children In Need* in the Midlands for the last eight years but tonight my job is given to Jo Malin who does a perfectly good job but lacks the sparkle I always gave the show.

I feel very alone tonight, no one to talk to, no one to just be there, it is very strange.

Lights out 10.30pm to the sound of a neighbouring cell playing indy music loudly, good job I kept hold of my earplugs.

Saturday 21st Nov.

Wake at 8.20am after the first decent night's sleep in weeks. Manage to speak to Jess at 10.30am she is pleased to hear about my new sleeping arrangements.

Back at my cell, unlocking my door with my own key there is a newspaper waiting, this is like heaven compared to what I've experienced during the last three weeks. I lie on my bed reading and watching TV. The peace is occasionally interrupted with inmates passing by to peer through the observation window in my cell door, I am the new tourist attraction once again.

Sunday 22nd Nov.

Wake at 8.15am, I have a headache, neck and shoulders in pain. I decide to give breakfast a miss and I'm not interested in taking any exercise. I'm happy to just keep myself to myself. An officer expresses concern that I haven't been out of my cell much during my two days here, and I explain that I'm happy to just have my own space and that I want to avoid the usual inquisitive questioning of people trying to get to know me.

2.30pm I take a shower and return to my cell to read. My peace is interrupted as usual, this time I'm paid a visit from a classmate called Narif, a twenty-four year old Asian guy from Wolverhampton. He's been here for over a year and has decided to take me under his wing. He is very knowledgeable about prison life and offers to give me anything I need. He tells me that my move to D-wing has caused concern among other inmates who believe I'm being shown favouritism.

Monday 23rd Nov

Monday is cookery day in class and the ingredients today include minced beef, I decide I'm going to cook a cottage pie. By 10.30am I am proud to produce a tasty looking crispy topped cottage pie. Others use their ingredients to make burgers. We sit and eat what we've cooked, but cottage pie at 10.30 on a Monday morning is not for me. Hilary invites a neighbouring class to join us and soon my offering is devoured, leaving me feeling proud as it is the first meal I've cooked for anyone in three months.

The classroom session this afternoon is spent looking at bank accounts and how to correctly complete a cheque, I just go along with it.

5.00pm, queue for dinner; faggots, boiled potatoes, mushy peas, it would've been piping hot but as I make my way back to my cell to eat I am held back as around ten officers run from all directions to deal with a fight which has broken out in the cell next to mine.

6.30pm, association, I am in the routine of showering and calling Jess. Then I return to my cell. On the way I notice a female officer struggling with a large box, I offer to lend a hand which she accepts, I carry the box as she unlocks gates, we end up in the segregation block, a separate section to D-Wing and my first glimpse of what *The Seg'* looks like. There are around fifteen single cells with nothing more than a bed and toilet. This can be home for anyone who refuses to follow the rules. It's a very lonely place. It turns out the box I am carrying contains the belongings of the inmate who's been involved in the earlier fight. He's earned himself a long stay in The Block.

Tuesday 24th Nov

Class today is particularly hard. There is an atmosphere created by Delroy Smithen. He is sulking and behaving like a pre-school child because the tutor Hilary refused to give him an extra portion of food in

207

yesterday's class. It makes the session drag and brings everyone's mood down. It only takes one bad apple.

During this evening's association I take the usual shower. The showers on D-Wing are communal rather than individual cubicles. In it there was a middle aged man who recognized me as being from the telly. He begins a bizarre conversation something along the lines of;

"I didn't expect to be standing next to a naked newsreader".

I guess he'll forever remember this time and no doubt get plenty of mileage down his local pub, I just hope he's generous when the inevitable question is asked.

I speak to Jess for half an hour on the phone, she's unable to visit this week as she's landed a job at the *Good Food Show*.

On my way back to my cell a chap by the name of Taffy is keen to chat to me. Taffy is fifty-one years old and he's coming to the end of a seven year sentence for armed robbery. It's not his first time in prison, he tells me he's spent thirty-three of his fifty-one years behind bars but he's had enough and won't be coming back. He plans to write a book.

Back in my cell I'm paid a visit by four inmates, they want me to store the Christmas Hooch. Hooch is a homemade alcoholic beverage using orange juice and yeast smuggled from the kitchen. It takes weeks to ferment and needs somewhere warm. They reckon I'm the least likely inmate to receive a cell search so would I store it? I decline.

Wednesday 25th Nov

Today's classroom subject is entitled The Family Man. We are encouraged to talk about the kind of family we each grew up in. A sensitive subject for many but to my surprise the group discusses it openly and with maturity, something I haven't yet seen in this class.

In the afternoon classroom session the group reverts to type and the class descends into the all too familiar juvenile behaviour. I become the target of Delroy Smithen's bullying as he decides he wants to convince the class that I'm not a celebrity. Not that I consider I am, but for some reason he feels a certain jealousy towards me all of a sudden. I defend myself the only way I know how to and that's with humour. Trouble is to understand my humour you have to have a certain level of intelligence, I am in a no-win situation.

I am relieved when class is over and I can return to the sanctuary of my small, cold cell.

I receive a visit from a chap called Ray, a Salvation Army officer who works in the chapel. He comes to pass on regards from the outside, he is friends with my BBC boss Liz Cave and her family, and is keen to ensure I am doing okay.

During association this evening I decide to socialize around the snooker table. There is a lot of banter and the mood is upbeat. They are welcoming and sympathetic, they've followed my story and feel that I've been harshly treated because of who I am.

Just before my door is locked for the night Delroy Smithen, the classroom bully comes to see me. He tells me that he's been chatting to others who are of the opinion that I am being given an easy time because of my celebrity status and that he's explained to them that it isn't my fault. There is no evidence of this being the case, however, it is their opinion and there is little I can do to change it. I am confused why Delroy has chosen to tell me this, but I guess it is his way of apologizing for his earlier behaviour towards me in the classroom.

Thursday 26th Nov.

Nothing of interest to report this day.

Friday 27th Nov.

I wake at exactly the same time as yesterday, 7.31am. This is like the film Groundhog Day. Attend class to learn how to write an effective CV. Going through the motions I complete mine in ten minutes, and using my very creative writing skills I help other classmates produce theirs. I enjoy the challenge of making serial offenders CV's interesting reading, and I'm very keen to know if, in the future, they are able to secure an interview based on it.

Half day today. The afternoon is spent in my cell until canteen arrives around

2.30pm. All present and correct, I have goodies for the week to keep a vague smile on my face. While collecting my booty, an officer tells me to expect a visit from an officer off G-Wing. I can't help but become excited at the prospect of moving to the super enhanced wing. Back in my cell I don't bother to pack away my new purchases in anticipation of my move. I wait all afternoon on tenterhooks, but by 7.00pm no one has been. I put my anticipation on hold for the night, maybe I'll be moving tomorrow. There's no association tonight which means no shower, but more sadly I don't get to speak to Jess.

I spend the evening replying to the steady stream of letters still arriving. I also study a prison document called an *OASYS* Report. This report is part of my prison record and risk assessment. It uses a scoring system, the higher the score, the more of a risk you are. Out of a possible 168 points my score is just 15, I'm, unsurprisingly, a very low risk. This is looking good for my HDC in April.

Saturday 28th Nov.

Door is unlocked for breakfast at 8.30, then again at 10.30 for association. I phone Jess who sounds very upbeat. We catch up, not really reporting anything, but it is good to hear her voice. I take a shower and return to my cell where I read and watch TV for much of the day. Still no one comes to take me to G-Wing. The peace of the afternoon is interrupted with the sound of alarm bells and officers rushing past my cell door. I can't quite see what is going on, but the commotion concludes with a prisoner being carried by six officers to the segregation block which is next door to my cell. Lights out 12 midnight.

Sunday 29th Nov.

8.10, woken up by the usual jangling of keys. Give breakfast and the first association a miss today, and my door remains locked. Am visited by two classmates who are keen to know why I am not out socializing. I explain that I'm not in the mood to mingle and that I'll be out later to shower and phone my loved one.

Lunch today is traditional roast beef, roast potatoes, sprouts and mash, rhubarb crumble and custard for dessert.

2.00pm, the door is unlocked for afternoon association, I shower and make my usual appointment to phone Jess. She's working so therefore I have to call her mobile, my credit is being eaten at the rate of a penny a second so the conversation is brief, but worthwhile to hear her voice. During our conversation she tells me that she'd driven past the prison last night on her way to see a friend who lives just ten minutes away. As she drove past the prison walls she began to cry. So near yet so far.

On the way back to my cell Taffy stops to chat, I learn from him that the commotion yesterday was Officer Motram being attacked. Mr. Motram has been very pleasant to me so I'm surprised when Taffy tells me the officer has a split personality which switches with the blink of an eye.

I return to my cell leaving inmates and officers socializing, playing pool, darts, scrabble and cards in a very calm atmosphere.

214

Monday 30th Nov.

Cookery in class today. Narif, Geordie, Lee and I are cooking prawn fried rice, a good team effort. An inmate called Steve Walker is nicked for refusing to work, all over a very childish fall out with the tutor Hilary. I learn that today would have been Hilary's mother's birthday so she's quite emotional and becomes upset. I react the only way I know how, and put my arm around her and offer to make a cup of tea. This would be normal behaviour in the outside world, but in prison I'm running the risk of being nicked myself for perhaps being over familiar. It is not my intention to be, but it's my instinct to help and to comfort if someone's upset.

The group sits and eats what we've cooked. A discussion starts about stereo systems in prison. Inmates are allowed to purchase stereo systems for their cell if they're Enhanced status. It's common on the wings for various stereo systems to compete for whose is the loudest, or who's got the latest music release. Often the wing reverberates with the echo of competing systems, it's hard to make out one particular song, it's just an annoying racket. I suggest inmates

215

should consider using headphones then they can listen to their own music as loudly as they like without disturbing everyone else. This suggestion is met with disgust and anger, I am shouted down by several members of our group as if I've suggested something sinister. No one in prison seems to want to compromise, the majority is selfish beyond belief, it seems a common trait in here, I'm going to have to learn to keep my suggestions to myself.

After lunch an officer tells me that I have completed my V.O. (Visiting Order) wrongly and it will be sent back to me. This means my planned visit by Jess won't take place this week.

During association this evening I learn more about the attack on officer Motram. Apparently an inmate threatened to climb onto the roof if he didn't get what he wanted, his attitude didn't sit right with the officer and a tussle ensued, the officer called for assistance and during the fight another officer's nose got blooded, all very dramatic.

I speak to Jess who's upset, she's been desperately trying to book a visit and has spent the afternoon hitting the redial button to the one and only clerk in the prison who deals with visits. It's so frustrating as we don't know when we'll get to see each other next.

Tuesday 1st Dec.

Wake at 7.45am shivering, the outside temperature has dropped to minus five overnight, it feels more like minus ten in my cell. I have two pipes running along the wall at floor level under the window which are supposed to heat the cell, however, the pipes have only ever gotten luke-warm and any heat radiated from them is sucked straight out of the ill-fitting, barred window.

In class we receive results of a test we completed yesterday. Two people completely failed and will have to re-sit, the average is 75%, I scored 100%. During a break for the library, classmate Ben Minton gets his thumb trapped in the steel gate as it is being slammed shut by an officer. From the classroom I hear a scream of agony, it is one of those screams that instantly tells you someone needs help. Hilary and I instinctively react and run out to see what has happened. I find Ben in the gents' toilet screaming in severe pain, blood gushing from his right hand. I hold his hand and see his thumb has been cut at the knuckle and is bleeding heavily. He is reeling in agony. I grab some toilet tissue, apply pressure to stem the bleeding, raise his arm and sit Ben down. I stay with him using humour to take his mind off the pain and gaping wound, while Hilary radios for the nurse.

During the afternoon classroom session we learn that Ben has been taken to hospital, his thumb has been broken.

Wednesday 2nd Dec.

I wake at 4.30am with thoughts of my incarceration running round my head which I desperately try to put from my mind. Not sure when I drifted back to sleep but I re-awake at 8.07am.

In class today we have a new tutor, a young black woman called Seana. It is her job to engage the group in a discussion about family members, the role they play within the family unit, and how internal and external factors can impact and lead to conflict within the household. An interesting exploration.

During lunch a dream I'd had during the night is drip fed back to me. I vaguely remember dreaming that heroin was being injected into my big toe! Bizarre, especially when you consider I have never in my life dreamt of drug use, let alone injecting heroin. I am becoming a product of my environment.

1.45pm back to the class to be educated on food hygiene and labeling. Cath, the tutor is being supervised by an inspector as part of her ongoing role within the prison service. I can't help but feel the pressure she must be under controlling this class. After an hour and half the inspector leaves to write up his report on the tutor's abilities in front of some of the worst students I've ever met. However, Cath seems to think it went well. As a thank you gesture for being so *well behaved*, Cath opens a box of PG Tips tea bags for class to have afternoon tea. Within seconds of the box being opened the contents of forty tea bags is reduced to just eight. Selfish filling of pockets by my classmates behaving more like vultures.

Cath realizes what's going on, but there's little she can do.

Dinner this evening is liver and onions followed by a small tub of Raspberry ice cream. I phone Jess, the mood of the conversation is down. I've been in prison for three months to the day and it's a real strain on us both. Despite that Jess does a great job of keeping what's left of any spirit up. The prospect of spending Christmas away from each other is daunting. If I can just get Christmas out of the way then perhaps we'll both feel much better.

I get my head down around 11.30pm, but I'm prevented from sleeping by loud music echoing from a cell opposite until 1.00am.

Thursday 3rd Dec.

There is a lot of noise on the wing as I wake up this morning, more than usual. Turns out the prison computer system has been updated and went live today, trouble is it's been experiencing a few glitches, for example not paying prisoners correct wages, and, more importantly, in some cases the new system has added as much as three days to inmate's sentences. Luckily not for me, however, my spending account balance has risen from £44 to £54, so no complaints there.

9.00am I'm off to class to amble through CV writing and fake job applications. I help others to complete theirs. It is amusing to say the least when it comes to the previous employment section of the fake forms, I don't think a job title such as armed blagger/bank robber is going to get the applicant a favourable response!

As I return to the wing this evening I am called into the office by senior officer Miss Lewis to inform me that she has spoken to G-Wing, and I am to expect a visit from Officer Hancock tomorrow, a space on the super enhanced wing has become available. Though excited at the prospect I decide not to get my hopes up too much, I've been here before only to be disappointed when no one arrives.

During association I phone Jess as usual who has some great news for a change. The payment protection insurance from a loan I'd repaid has been refunded, a cheque for almost six thousand pounds is on its way, the refund will help pay off my mounting debts. Jess has been battling with my creditors since I've been in prison, what I'd have done without her God only knows. This injection of money will help appease my debtors for a while at least.

Friday 4th Dec.

The classroom session is very relaxed today, we're coming to the end of the nine week course and somehow much of the curriculum has been completed, either that or the tutor for this session Michael Bridges has given up on the wayward group.

Delroy Smithen takes the floor to tell us about his crime career, armed robbery for which it netted the gang of four 50k each, he received six years. He's coming to the end of his sentence in February and claims he'll never return to his old ways, he jokingly says he's going to target celebrities instead of banks, and I can't help thinking many a true word is spoken in jest.

Nafir, the nucleus of the group, (two years GBH and robbery), is also coming to the end of his sentence in February. Both share a nervousness about the prospect of being released, and wonder how they're going to cope with life on the outside. It's apparent to me that they've become institutionalized.

11.45am class dismisses for the weekend. During the walk back to the wing Nafir pulls me to one side and asks who I'm paying protection money to. He tells me there's a rumour that I'm paying for a body guard to keep an eye on me. Needless to say this is news to me.

Back at my cell the first of the Christmas cards is waiting from my eldest sister Cheryl, lovely words but as far as I'm concerned Christmas is cancelled this year.

I watch the lunch time edition of BBC *Midlands Today*, this helps me to feel a connection to my old life. It's presented by my good friend, Nick Owen, who reports the release of a film called *Nativity* in which I play a part. The film has hit box office records in the first weekend of release. Needless to say I don't get to go to the premiere and I won't be there to celebrate its success.

Saturday 5th Dec.

I am woken this morning at 5.30am, first by an officer switching my light on from outside the cell and peering through the observation window. He checks that I haven't made good my escape during the night, or decided to string myself up from the window bars in a suicide attempt. Then half an hour later by a second officer who has squeaky footwear and is whistling loudly. He does exactly the same thing as the first. I get the impression from this officer that he feels, because he is up at an ungodly hour, then so should everyone else. He makes no attempt to be quiet, in fact quite the opposite.

Wide awake at this point I get up turn on the TV, and shave. I watch rolling news of the murder of Meredith Kercher. Amanda Knox has been found guilty and she's been sentenced to twenty-six years in prison. Her parents are appealing and wonder how the justice system could have behaved so badly. I have some empathy with her situation. Her parents are calling it a miscarriage of justice, I draw similarities with my own case though mine did not involve premeditated murder.

224

While thinking about being away from Jess this morning a famous quote by La Rochefoucauld drops into my mind and instantly picks me up;

"Absence diminishes mediocre passions and increases great ones, just as the wind extinguishes candles but fans a fire".

This is certainly true in our case, Jess is doing a great job of keeping our relationship alive while we're apart and constantly delivers the reassurance I so desperately need on a daily basis. Thank you sweetheart.

9.20a.m., Officer Jones stops by to ask if I want to exercise, I decline and he stays for a chat. He sympathizes with my situation by saying it could happen to anyone and that I am a victim of circumstance. He asks about my general well-being, and mentions that there's a vacancy for a cleaner in the segregation block. He is looking for someone trustworthy for the role and would be happy to consider me if I am interested. I am flattered to be considered trustworthy enough, and I thank him for the offer. We are joined by a young officer, Mr. Sampson. Very pleasant, and he agrees that I would be ideal for the job, and between the three of us we agree that I will be offered the job when my education course comes to an end in three weeks' time.

10.30, association, I talk to Jess on the phone, she's in a great mood having had a meeting with our accountant, she assures me that my financial affairs or problems are in good hands.

I clean my cell from top to bottom and spend the afternoon writing letters, I'm forced to stop when my pen runs dry, and I am unable to get another one until we're unlocked for dinner at around 4.45pm.

Burger, boiled potatoes, yogurt for dessert. I swap today's copy of The *Mirror* with Delroy Smithen for two half-filled biros, which means I'm able to continue to reply to letters, and write this diary throughout the long hours locked up over the weekend.

Sunday 6th Dec.

Awake at 8.00am and I decline a cooked breakfast, exercise and association at 10.30. Instead I stay in my cell to answer a letter from a friend who has lots of questions about what life is like on the inside. That takes me up to lunch time. Something resembling turkey, mashed potatoes, roast potatoes and sprouts is slopped onto my plastic dinner plate. In my blue plastic bowl; jam roll with the option of custard.

2.30, during association I speak to Jess, only briefly however, as she's on her mobile which eats my credit at an astonishing rate. All is well.

I take a shower and bang myself up to watch TV and write. I'm interrupted by a visit from a guy called Wilson who works on the servery ladling custard or gravy. It's a passing social visit, he's concerned that I choose to stay in my cell rather than socialize. I point out that I'm not keen to make any friends here, and as long as I can use the phone and shower every day then I'm okay with that, no offence intended. He tells me he's overheard officers talking about my move to G Wing and he reckons I'll be there soon. I won't hold my breath.

Monday 7th Dec

Eyes open at 7.47am, attend cookery class at 8.45 where I bake a delicious treacle sponge.

227

Back to the wing for lunch where I'm greeted by senior officer Miss Lewis who has a letter for me to sign. It's from a good friend, Eddie Hughes, a Walsall Conservative councillor. He's been in touch with the prison via email to confirm my whereabouts.

While I'm in the office Miss Lewis is confused as to why I haven't gone to G Wing yet, she tells me she's spoken to them several times and they are waiting to accept me, but the Number One Governor, Mr. Small, is concerned that I haven't met my targets. When I explain that I am unaware of any targets that I have to achieve, she makes a phone call to the Offender Management Unit. This is a department within the prison which looks after an inmate's prison records. Often when a prisoner is sent to jail there are certain conditions that have to be adhered to as part of their incarceration and rehabilitation process, for example; if I had a problem with drink or drug use then I would have to attend a course to deal with the issue and be awarded a certificate to show that I have successfully participated in the rehabilitation of my behaviour.

The phone call confirms that no such targets have been set and therefore I should be able to progress through the system without any trouble. I'm told the next available space on G Wing is the 19th or the 21st December and hopefully this will all be sorted by then. Miss Lewis agrees that it's only because I'm famous that I'm having such difficulty progressing and the Governor does not want to appear to be fast tracking me. It seems I'm being lionized, fame is working against me once again. While I'm in the office several of my classmates spot me and are intrigued as to what maybe going on, no doubt they'll have questions and allegations for me later.

1.45pm back to class for Christmas card making. Never a big fan of sending Christmas cards and seeing as I've decided Christmas is cancelled this year I choose not to make one, but instead offer my assistance to anyone who needs help with theirs.

As I expected I am grilled about my appearance in the office during lunch time, and when I decline to comment the group becomes more suspicious and upset with me. To appease them I come clean and tell them it is about my move to G Wing. They become even more upset, and begin an argument about me receiving privileged treatment. I try to point out that because of who I am it's the exact opposite and my progression is being hindered, but they are having none of it. Envy in prison, as with many emotions, is much more prevalent. I put it down to hyper-sensitivity and emotion. I decide I need to be more aloof and leave them to think about what they want, I'm in a no-win situation again.

6.15, association. I shower and speak to Jess on the phone. It's only a brief conversation as for the next couple of days she'll be working into the evening and only available on her mobile. However brief our conversations are Jess always reassures me that everything is fine which means I'm able to spend another night in this God forsaken place in the knowledge that my Jess is okay. No wish to socialize as I make my way back to my cell when I bump into Taff. He's grinning from ear to ear as he's going home tomorrow after seven and a half years here. What a fantastic feeling he must be experiencing to be going home especially just before Christmas. I feel a certain amount of envy myself as I shake his hand

and wish him the best of luck. Lights out 11.30pm.

Tuesday 8th Dec

Wake at 7.53am, there's no class today, we will be locked up for much of the day due to staff training. So I expect to have a very quiet day but despite the lock-down there's a lot of movement on the landing and I get a visit from Steve Walker a classmate. He wants the crossword from yesterday's paper. Twenty minutes later a neighbouring inmate knocks my cell door asking for sugar, as neighbours do. Another fifteen minutes goes by and Miss H, the senior officer, unlocks my door to deliver today's newspaper and to pass on a message that Dave and Christine Hart (my BBC *Midlands Today* boss and his wife) have telephoned the prison to speak to me which is definitely not allowed, but nice try. They enquired about my well-being and asked whether I was behaving myself, it is a kind gesture, and very kind of Miss H to pass on the message. Another half hour passes and my next visitor is Elliot, he's the Number One on the wing, and the first guy to welcome me here three weeks ago. He asks whether I'd like to join a team in a computer game

231

tournament for Christmas, when I confess I'm useless at computer games we agree that I'll be more of a hindrance than an asset to his team. He stays for a chat through the locked door and reassures me that if there's any problem, or anything I need, then I'm to let him know. Elliot is a tall, good looking, mixed race guy of about twenty-seven years of age. He keeps a quiet confidence about him, and runs D wing well with a high respect from all the other inmates. I have no idea what he's here for, and I'm intrigued to find out.

Visiting continues, this time it is from another classmate, Nafir, who is complaining to me about Delroy Smithen. They have clearly fallen out about something, and I am happy to be the listening post.

6.20pm, association, when I have my usual appointment to hear my sweetheart's voice. I shower and return to my cell. I am happy when the wing falls relatively silent at around 10.30pm. Another day done.

Weds 9th Dec.

7.53am get myself together to attend class at 8.45am. Today we're discussing family issues. The session includes a very heated discussion, mainly between Delroy Smithen and myself. He is in a very bad mood over his fall out with Nafir, and is paranoid that Nafir has confided in me. He is concerned that we are both conspiring against him, and he sees me as a threat. He decides to remark that I am not a celebrity, and I am nothing but a weatherman. When I try to explore where his problem with me is coming from he becomes angry and more aggressive with his use of words towards me. I am keen to ensure that despite his temper I won't appear to be frightened or intimidated by his behaviour. He continues to air his concerns in front of the class of eight and the tutor Seana. His concerns are, in his words;

"Why do I cower in my cell? Why do I run back to my cell and not choose to socialize during Association? Why am I scared to mix?"
His opinion is that I consider myself to be better than them because I choose not to mingle. When I try to explain that I prefer

233

my own company and that I'm trying to get through this sentence in my own way he seems to become even more angry and wound up. It becomes clear to me that he wants to resolve this in the only way he knows how, and that's by punching me. The tutor also recognizes this, and intervenes to try to calm Delroy down, but by now he's wound himself up that much he is accepting no one's point of view but his own. There is no point arguing with him any longer so I decide to remain quiet and leave the tutor to do the talking until we break for lunch. As we walk back to the wing Delroy chooses to walk ahead and alone. I decide the best thing to do is to keep away from him.

The afternoon classroom session is conducted within a strained atmosphere, Delroy and I having decided not to speak to one another.

6.20, association. I shower, during which I'm told that I have just been on the news about my failed appeal, seems it's only just been leaked. I speak to Jess who isn't happy, her phone has been ringing since my latest appearance on the box, but it's no shock to us as we knew about this a month ago. We reaffirm our love and say goodbye, I'll be seeing her tomorrow when she pays a visit.

I return to my cell to find my door has been locked by an officer, this means I will have to socialize until he returns. Not a problem until I spot Delroy looking at me playing pool, and believing he is responsible for forcing me out of my cell at last.

What a day, lights out 10.35.

Thursday 10th Dec.

In class today our task is to practice writing job applications including disclosure of our time spent at Her Majesties pleasure.

Jess pays a visit this afternoon, great to see her. She brings me up to date with my financial situation, and moves onto her job prospects. It is a great visit albeit too short. Before I know it I am back in my cell sitting on the edge of my bed thinking how lucky I am to have Jess who has kept me strong throughout this ordeal.
6.20pm, association. I phone Jess who's just got through the door after her eighty mile round trip to visit me. I reaffirm how great

it was to see her and thank her for standing by me throughout, her response is;
"Don't be silly".

I go for a shower to find Delroy Smithen already in full lather. To break the atmosphere we begin a conversation about Christmas and his soon-after release. This is the first time we've spoken to each other since our heated fall out. After we run out of small talk Delroy offers an apology for his behaviour towards me yesterday. I reach over to shake his hand which seems inappropriate seeing as we're both in the buff, but I feel it is the right thing to do. I return my own apology, and we put the whole thing behind us.

Back to my cell to answer letters and reflect on what has turned into a good day, thanks to the magic of Jess's visit.

Friday 11th Dec.

At school today we do nothing but watch a DVD, *Hannibal*, it is the first time the whole class's attention is focused.
Half day on Friday, the usual kit change and canteen delivered during the afternoon, then banged up for the rest of the evening.

Saturday 12th Dec.

Awake at 7.54am, decline cooked breakfast and exercise. Association at 10.15, I sweep and mop my tiny abode, which takes all of five minutes.

I order the next four weeks supply of daily newspapers costing me £11.60. I have to be careful, my spends account is running low, and although Jess has sent a cheque, I'm told that it could take up to four weeks to clear through the prison's banking system and then is credited to my account. This will leave me with no funds over the Christmas period, not that I need to buy Christmas presents, but it would be good to have money in my account for a few goodies and credit for the phone to keep me upbeat throughout the long periods of being locked away.

In prison there are bad days, and days that aren't so bad. Today I'm having a bad day. I'm feeling down and depressed so I try to keep myself to myself. During the afternoon a pile of letters and Christmas cards is delivered. Wonderful friends are still taking the time to think about me and drop me a line with words of kindness and

237

support. Reading them reminds me of how much I miss my friends, colleagues and my wonderful job. My mood descends deeper into depression. Enclosed in one envelope is a small pop up Christmas tree from a close friend with the words

"Saw this and thought of you, something to brighten up your cell at Christmas".

The trickle of tears I notice rolling down my cheek soon turns into a river drenching my face and the tiny table on which I'm writing this diary entry. I just about manage to pull myself together, and spend the evening replying to the letters.

During ITV's *X Factor* I watch a performance by Joe McEldery of Luther Vandros' song; *Dance With My Father Again*, this opens a floodgate of tears again. The song reminds me of my Mum. I cry a hurricane of tears at a photo I have of the remarkable woman with her arm around my son I have pinned on my cell wall.

The photo was taken the year she died, 2000. My son Calam, was only ten years old.

The picture was taken in the living room of the family home beneath a clock showing the time of 10.47am. Mum is wearing a silver wig as, through Chemotherapy, she lost her hair. Despite the pain she must be feeling and the knowledge of knowing she was dying she still manages to smile that gorgeous smile which I miss so much seeing on her beautiful, loving face. A smile which I am pleased to have inherited.

At this time I'm feeling the most depressed, the most miserable that I've felt since coming to jail. Is it finally getting to me? Is it because Christmas is around the corner? What is it? Today is a bad day, a very bad day.

Sunday 13th Dec

Wake at 8.00am, am unlocked at 10.00am and taken along with seven other inmates to the reception block to pick up a parcel. It is a writing pad and envelopes sent by Liz Goddard, a colleague from the BBC, a very sweet and kind gesture, very typical of Liz. Prison rules mean I'm not allowed to keep the gift. The package will be placed in my personal belongings where it will remain until I'm released.

Quiet Sunday spent the evening replying to letters. Joe McEldery won X Factor, and Ding won the UK Snooker Championship. Lights out midnight.

Monday 14th Dec.

Wake up 8.16am. Education at 8.45, today, we are to complete a Level Two Food Hygiene course with a forty minute exam this afternoon. My usual class has swelled to fifteen as another class doing the same course has joined us under one tutor. This means new faces that aren't used to being in such close proximity to me, and the usual banter ensues. It is light-hearted and the new group is very nice and sympathetic toward me.

11.45 am, break for lunch. Leek and Potato soup with chips, and a jam doughnut for dessert.

1.45pm return to the class. Pinky (gambler) brings a copy of the Birmingham Mail with the headlines, "Ashley loses appeal", and a photograph of me looking forlorn. The presence of the paper subjects me to more banter from the group which labels me a child batterer. The article has left me feeling angry at the victim's comments, and the fact that he refuses to accept any responsibility for what happened. The newspaper continues its attack on me, but being a journalist I understand that I'm a great story for them to sell newspapers. My instinct is to fight back at the article, and it's frustrating not to have the option of responding, but I decide my time will come to put my side, and it's not while I'm in this place.

Nevertheless, I continue with my studies and pass the forty minute exam.

4.45pm, back to the wing for dinner. Faggots, green beans, and potatoes. Apple crumble for afters.

I keep a low profile during association, I shower, phone Jess, return to my cell to a pile of Christmas cards waiting to be opened, and put them on display in my tiny room. The usually dreary looking prison cell is looking more like a Christmas grotto by the day.

Tuesday 15th Dec.

Awake at 8.00am after a very restless night's sleep. In class today we have a *Ready Steady Cook* style challenge. Cook a tasty dish within an hour. I team up with Geordie, and we decide we're cooking an Indian dish of Keema & Peas with plain rice and home-made chapattis. It turns out to be delicious with plenty to go around, enough even for two officers who stop by to carry out random drugs tests. They each demolish a plate of Keema and rice, and congratulate us on our efforts.

11.45 break for lunch, during which Officer Badman (yes, that's her real name!) stops by to inform me that I cannot go to G Wing as I do not have anything on my sentence plan to aim for, no rehabilitation courses. I explain that it is not up to me to design a sentence plan it is up to the prison service, and that I will adhere to anything the prison service deems necessary for me to complete in order that I can move through the system. She informs me that it is always necessary to have something on a sentence plan in order that the prison service can monitor my progression and can be seen to have played its part in my rehabilitation. So, after lunch I miss education to attend an interview with Officer Badman to bring my prison file up to date, and assess me for any rehabilitative courses. My risk level currently stands at 15 out of a possible 168, once we've completed the update it is likely to be even lower than this. After an hour, the meeting concludes thus: Enhance Thinking Skills (ETS) programme, I don't meet the criteria, so I am declined. TSP (Thinking Skills Programme) I shall be assessed for but I am unlikely to meet the criteria. Anger Management Control, I shall be assessed for, but unlikely to qualify, blah, blah, blah, you get the gist. So then it is decided that perhaps I can make a valuable contribution during my incarceration by helping other prisoners with reading and writing, and by becoming a Listener. Officer Badman is very helpful and goes out of her way to update my file as soon as possible so that I can begin to move through the system. She also advises me on Home Detention Curfew, and Category D applications and procedures. Not all of what she tells me sounds good, but we agree that she'd rather be straight with me than create false hope. I'm grateful for her honesty. I leave the meeting with the distinct impression that the prison system doesn't get many prisoners like me, and by that very nature I am being singled out as unique, and it's working against me.

Back in my cell I write a letter to my probation officer to bring him up to date with our meeting and any concerns that have arisen.

Weds 16th Dec.

My afternoon classroom session is interrupted by two young ladies from the prison's psychology department. No doubt fresh off their psychology degree from the local uni', the two youngsters hand me a clipboard with twenty-nine questions exploring whether I would become angry and violent at the drop of a hat. The result of this short test will determine whether I qualify for an Anger Management course. The test isn't exactly scientific. I complete the assessment whilst standing just outside the classroom in the small corridor within seven minutes. I'm told I will be notified of the results by this coming Friday and return to the classroom to answer a barrage of questions by my nosey classmates who just want to know whether I'm getting something that they're not.

After dinner a pile of post is delivered to my cell, mainly Christmas cards from colleagues, and a letter from an inmate at Winson Green, Darren Matto a millionaire family businessman from the Black Country. I got on extremely well with Darren during my eight weeks at the Green. He is shorter than me at about 5'6", but he's stocky, is as hard as nails, and stands for "nothing from no one" as he once said to me. It is good to hear from him.

During association this evening I am told by classmate Steve Walker that a particular officer has taken a dislike to me for no reason. Steve is giving me the heads up and advises me to avoid Officer Phoenix. He tells me that he has overheard Officer Phoenix saying that if he has anything to do with it I won't be going to G Wing. This news comes as a surprise to me as Officer Phoenix hasn't been anything but professional in his rare dealings with me, I am certainly not of the impression that I have upset him in anyway. Steve usually speaks his mind and is not one for idle gossip so there's no reason for me to disbelieve him. I return to my cell to consider this new piece of information, and decide to monitor the relationship between Phoenix and myself.

Jess is visiting tomorrow and I'm looking forward to seeing her so much. Lights out 12.30am

Thursday 17th Dec.

In class today we do nothing but watch
another film, *The Godfather*. Seems to me
that with the combination of Christmas
around the corner, and the tutor's lack of
control of his unruly pupils, the easiest
option is to just kick back. Having seen *The
Godfather* a number of times I decide to
concentrate my attention on an article
written in The Sun newspaper by a former
boss of mine, Kelvin McKenzie. He is
commenting on the jailing of Munir
Hussain, a businessman who attacked a
burglar at his home. The case has
similarities to my own, however, The Sun
has reported his case in favour of him,
defending his actions for protecting his
property. I decide to make notes for when
I meet the editor of the *Birmingham Mail*,
Steve Dyson, to ask why his reporters seem
to have it in for me. Shortly after I was
jailed the paper ran an article asking its
readers to write in with their thoughts on
my sentence. Around eight out of ten were
in support of my actions and could
sympathize with my situation. So why does
the paper choose to take this line with me?
I'm keen to find out, and have a strong urge
to write to Steve with my thoughts, but I

fear he may print my letter and, while I'm here, I will have no recourse to defend myself. It's frustrating, but I have to be patient.

1.55pm I'm taken from my cell on D Wing the short distance to the visits block where Jess is waiting having made her weekly pilgrimage to HMP Stafford. Visits procedure is running well behind today because the Governor decided to give his staff an extra half hour for lunch in order to carry out last minute Christmas shopping. This has caused uproar among the thirty-five prisoners who are looking forward to seeing their loved ones, for some this will be the last time they get to see their family before Christmas. I sympathize with their anger, but the officers on duty just shrug off their protests.

I'm eventually allowed through at around 2.30pm to see a slightly stressed Jess waiting at table 31. Her car wouldn't start so she opted to catch the train at the last minute. Nevertheless we both settle down and begin to enjoy our short time together. We discuss what we should do about how the *Birmingham Mail* is reporting my story and she agrees she will speak to Steve

Dyson. Jess and I bring each other up to date with everything that has happened during the last week, and before we know it our time is up, and I am being herded back to my cell.

My cell has turned bitterly cold as the first of the winter's snow falls, and an icy wind blows, whistling between the bars on the window. I use toilet tissue as draft excluder, and towels as curtains to slow the icy draft, it's going to be a very cold night.

Post is pushed under my door by an anonymous delivery man, included in the pile of Christmas cards is my Level 2 Food Hygiene Certificate.

The Highfield

LEVEL 2
Food Safety
Certificate

This is to certify that

Mr. Ashley Blake

has successfully completed a Level 2 **Food Safety Course** of 6 hours' duration

Subjects covered:

→ Introduction to food safety
→ Microbiological hazards
→ Food poisoning and its control
→ Contamination hazards and controls
→ HACCP from purchase to service
→ Personal hygiene
→ Food premises and equipment
→ Food pests and control
→ Cleaning and disinfection
→ Food safety law and enforcement

Signed on behalf of _____ *Manchester College*

14th December 2009

Course Date

Materials provided by Highfield.co.uk

Richard A. Sprenger
Managing Director
Highfield.co.uk ltd

Quality, Value, Service & Integrity

Highfield
.co.uk limited

The UK's leading supplier of food safety and health & safety training materials and training

www.highfield.co.uk

2

6.20, association. I speak to Jess to ensure she's arrived home safely.

On my way back to my cell I am stopped by a large, black guy who asks me for advice on writing a book. I am happy to offer what advice I can, but having never written a book in my life my advice is general. I soon realize that his request for advice is just a ruse in order that he can question me in depth about my finances. He is convinced I am a multi-millionaire, and it takes a while to try to convince him otherwise. After about twenty minutes the questioning is, thankfully, interrupted by Elliot, who tells the big, black guy, who by now has me cornered, that he is asking too many personal questions, and he is to leave me be. Thank you Elliot.

Friday 18th Dec.

3.37am, the cold of the cell wakes me up. My nose, the only body part protruding from beneath my 13.5 tog duvet, is colder than a polar bear's. I watch TV for a while. Not sure what time I drifted off, but I wake again at 7.51am.

The subject in class today is ... watching another DVD. This time *Alien*, during which a heated argument erupts because Paddy, a small Irish guy, is talking over the film. The argument almost turns to fisticuffs as voices try to outdo one another. I witness the most childish behaviour so far on the course, I put this down to festive frustrations, boredom and heaps of anger.

After lunch I am unlocked by Officer Morgan and taken to the office to be interviewed for a HOPIN (Helping Other Prisoners In Need) position. I'm asked several questions in the style of a job interview, and my answers are written down and assessed for my suitability for the role. My results will be passed to the prison's Labour Board for final assessment and approval. I'm shown a large photograph of me which will be placed on the wall outside my cell door to identify me to anyone who needs help with reading, writing, form filling and so on. Before I leave the office Miss Lewis updates me on my progress to G Wing. It's looking more likely to be the end of January I'm told and with my latest employment roles and responsibilities in my prison file there shouldn't be any problem, on paper I'm

252

every bit the model prisoner. In the meantime I'm offered a cell move as compensation, however, the cell on offer is right by the snooker table on the main landing where most of the inmates congregate during association, this would mean I'll be in the thick of it, a centre of attention, something I'm desperately keen to avoid. Although the cell is much warmer than mine, I politely decline the kind offer and stay put.

The result of my assessment for the Anger Management course is delivered and reports that I am not a suitable candidate for the course, a note will be made in my file to at least show I have made the approach.

MEMORANDUM

Thinking Skills
Programme

HMP Stafford

From:	Sarah Rowley	Date:	16th December 2009
	TSP Facilitator	Ref:	Ashley Blake
To:	Adele Badman	Number:	A3043AH
	Offender Supervisor		

We have received the referral for the above named person to be assessed for the Thinking Skills Programme.

Unfortunately, this person does not meet the initial criteria for the programme based on their level of risk and need.

Please contact a member of the TSP team if you have any further queries.

Regards,

Sarah Rowley
TSP Team

PSYCHOLOGICAL SERVICES DEPARTMENT

Anger Control Training Programme

To: Mr. Blake   **Number:** A3043AH

Wing: D1-19

Date: 17 December 2009

Dear Mr. Blake,

You have recently been assessed for the Anger Control Training Programme; however the outcome of this assessment indicated that you would not benefit from attending this programme.

This does not mean that you will not be suitable for other types of programmes designed to address anger issues and therefore you may be approached to be assessed for another programme.

A copy of this letter will be placed in your sentence planning file.

Regards,

pp Melanie Woolridge
ACT Treatment Manager

Cc: Sentence Planning

2.50pm, kit change and delivery of canteen. Always the highlight of the week, fresh clothing and bedding, and treats from the tuck shop. All of the items I ordered on my canteen sheet are present and correct apart from a plastic tin opener which means I'll be unable to get into two cans of tuna and a can of pineapple chunks for a little while longer. 5.00pm, early bang-up on Fridays. Watch TV and try to stay as warm as I can, but my nose is about to develop frostbite. Lights out 11.45pm

Saturday 19th Dec

Wake up at 8.30, the cell is freezing as the overnight temperature dropped to minus five degrees in Staffordshire. I try to remain in the relative warmth beneath my 13.5 tog duvet which has turned out to be the best purchase of my life, but there are constant interruptions: breakfast? Exercise? Got any papers? Got any burn? What are you up to? Going to the gym? Constant visitors, constant questions - LEAVE ME ALONE!!!

2.30pm, association. I speak to Jess who sounds really down and pissed off, despite my attempts I fail to cheer her up. I guess Christmas is not going to be very nice for her at all.

Officer Farnell delivers a bag of post, Christmas cards and letters in which I learn two of my best friends have each lost a parent to cancer. Rachel Bowering lost her Dad, and Gemma Moore lost her Mum, dreadful news. Having experienced the loss of my Mum to cancer I have been a source of support and sympathy to both my friends during their parents' battle over the last year, we've cried and laughed together and now I'm not there when they need me most, it's horrible, it's so cruel. I write letters, a pathetic alternative but the only option. Lights out 11.45pm

Sunday 20th Dec.

I write thank you letters all morning to as many people as have sent me Christmas cards, but I have a limited supply of postage stamps so I have to prioritize. I write a letter to Jess, a heart-felt letter for Christmas, setting out exactly how much I love her, and thanking her for sticking by me throughout this ordeal. I make several promises about our future and ask her to look forward to happier times ahead.

After lunch I speak to Jess on the phone. Shortly into our conversation the phone goes dead. I can't get her back. Each time I try an automated voice message tells me there is a fault with the line. After twenty minutes of trying I manage to get through, but again our conversation is cut short as I am being called to attend reception to pick up a parcel.

256

The parcel is from Jess. She sent it well over a week ago, it contains one of my flight ground school study books. There is also a gift-wrapped box containing a Stephen Fry book, *Moab Is My Washpot*. It is from my former boss Liz Cave, such a sweet and thoughtful present. It will help during the long Christmas period I'll be spending alone in my cell.

4.30pm dinner is served, breaded fish, baked potato, beans. Then the door is slammed and locked for the next fifteen hours.

Monday 21st Dec

Back to class at 8.45am. On the way an Asian chap runs over to hand me a copy of the front page of Friday 18th December edition of the *Birmingham Mail*, the headline reads;

BREWERY SELLS OFF ASHLEY BLAKE'S PUB.

Is this news? Does this really sell papers? More questions for the paper's editor.

In class today we're cooking a full English breakfast. This creates much excitement among my juvenile classmates who get on with the process with much enthusiasm, the incentive being a slap up breakfast at the end.

Back on the wing the Christmas canteen forms have been delivered for completion. I'm allowed to spend £48.23 over the entire period, there'll be no canteen next week so whatever I order has to last me until Friday 8th January 2010. I shop carefully and spend my money thoughtfully.

6.00pm, association. I speak to Jess who's spoken to Steve Dyson about concerns we have with the way he's reporting my story. Jess tells me she got on well with Steve who agreed to look at the coverage, and hopefully adjust it. He also expressed his desire to arrange a visit to see me face to face. Jess is in high spirits as we say our goodbyes.

I also phone my best mate Gez. I've only spoken to him once since being jailed, and it is great to hear his voice, although slightly slurred as he confesses to being pissed. He tells me that he's moving to Moscow, flight booked for the 12th January 2010, he's secured a job in the financial markets there. Although I'm pleased for him, I'm upset for me. He won't be there when I'm eventually released, we won't share many beers and stories. He becomes upset on the phone, a mixture of emotions and alcohol, in turn I become upset and fight to hold back tears. Nevertheless it is great to talk to *me old pal* who I desperately miss.

I get back to my cell trying to swallow a lump in my throat, and to digest all the information Jess and Gez have given me. I decide to pen a letter to Steve Dyson with my thoughts of his reporters, and what really happened that fateful night. It takes the whole evening.

Tuesday 22nd Dec

Today is very much the same as those last days at school in the run up to Christmas when no real class work is done. The teacher takes a very relaxed stance and allows the class to do what they want, play games, draw, chat, watch DVD's. Little did I know back then that I'd be doing the same at the age of forty one.

Wednesday 23rd Dec

The countdown to Christmas continues in the classroom. The tutor, Amerik, kindly brought in a jar of coffee and mince pies as a Christmas treat for the class to enjoy. The treats are devoured in seconds. Someone notices one of the ingredients of the festive mince pies is Brandy, although the tiniest amount, it is the first drop of alcohol I've ingested in four months. We play computer games and scrabble.

During the evening association I phone Jess, and then phone my son Calam. I am disappointed when his mobile phone goes to voicemail. I leave a message and remind him how much I miss and love him. It's the first time I've called him since coming to prison, we've communicated by letter and through Jess. I don't want him to visit and see his old man in a place like this.

The post is delivered and I'm overwhelmed with the amount of Christmas cards from colleagues and friends. It's heartwarming that people are still thinking about me, and taking the time and effort to send me Christmas cards and gifts, I'm very lucky.

Thursday 24th Dec Christmas Eve.

There's no class today we've broken up for the Christmas period. 10.45am there's a kit change during which prison officers hand out goody bags containing crisps, squash, biscuits and noodles, and wish us a Merry Christmas. It is like receiving a surprise Christmas stocking, and brings back fond memories of my childhood at Christmas when Mum would hang a stocking from my bedroom door handle. On Christmas morning as I turned the handle on my bedroom door I'd hear the clunk as the stocking, crammed full of sweets and chocolate, slipped off and hit the floor. I'd spend the whole morning gorging, as kids do.

Jess is visiting today. I'm excited but also very apprehensive. It'll be great to see her, but I'm worried about the feelings when it's time for her to leave. This will be the first Christmas in our six year relationship that we've been apart. I have no present for her, I won't be cooking her Christmas dinner, I won't get to see her excited little face as she opens presents. This is the nightmare I've been dreading ever since the judge announced my sentence back in September.

261

1.45pm, visiting is running late as it did last week, and instead of two hours with our loved ones on Christmas Eve our visiting time is reduced to just an hour. It upsets the inmates who are threatening to stage a sit in at the end of visiting.

Jess looks great as we sit down at table number 40. We have very little to talk about as we speak on the phone every day, but it's perfectly okay just to be in each other's company, and we manage to fill the little time we have by holding hands tightly, talking of our future wedding plans and holidays.

4.00pm, "finish off your visits" shouts an officer who would be a good contender for a sergeant major or town crier, his loud announcement makes the entire room jump resulting in some of the young children crying at the bad man.

Our goodbyes are long and stalled as neither of us wants to let go. We maintain eye contact as Jess walks towards the exit, blowing kisses and mouthing the words, *I love you*, with each step. One final kiss blown, and my sweetheart is gone.

It is at this point I most want to attempt an escape, even if only for twenty-four hours so I can be with Jess on Christmas Day. I use all my strength to hold back tears, I look around to see whether I can get some sort of indication of how I am supposed to behave in this situation. I can see a sea of men's faces who are all in the same boat as me.

As I am led back to my cell the stress and emotion of saying goodbye brings on a severe headache. I spend the evening in my cell, leaving once to call Jess to be sure she's gotten home safely and to thank her for coming to see. I watch TV feeling very sorry for myself. Lights out 11.00pm, but I am prevented from sleeping by the sound of 'window warriors' shouting obscenities at one another.

(Window warriors are prisoners who shout to one another from the window of their locked cell. Whole conversations and more often arguments are conducted by shouting through the small opening of the cell window. This means that the whole prison is part of the conversation or argument).

Friday 25th Dec, Christmas Day.

Woken at 8.15am by a very jolly Miss Hanlon and Miss Aston, both wearing Santa hats. My severe headache hasn't budged, and I am not in the mood for getting out of bed. The wing sounds jovial. I manage to get myself together, shave, and at least make an effort at some sort of Christmas.

10.00am, association. I phone my son Calam to wish him a Merry Christmas, but as usual it goes straight to voicemail. I phone Jess and we both manage to keep our tears of sadness out of the conversation, it would be too upsetting to hear. I take a shower and head for my cell. On the way I notice the nurse's hatch is open, a Godsend, the nurse gives me two packets of painkillers, Paracetamol and Ibuprofen, and advises me to take two of each every four to six hours.

My head hurts so badly I can't eat, I feel sick. The Christmas dinner has all the traditional trimmings, and by all accounts the kitchen has done the prisoners proud, but this means nothing to me as I give my offering away.

I spend Christmas Day evening in a freezing cold prison cell, in severe pain with a migraine. Today is what I've been dreading all along. I turn the lights and TV off at 7.30pm, and go to sleep.

Saturday 26th Dec Boxing Day

I am woken with the door being unlocked at 8.20am, still in severe pain in the left side of my head and neck, and feeling nauseous. I decline a cooked breakfast. I've taken the pain killers as directed but they have had little or no effect. I stay in bed reeling in pain throughout the morning.

2.30pm, I queue for thirty minutes to use the phone to call Jess. We chat for a while. Jess is pleased Christmas is over. I try to describe my previous twenty-four hours but can't find the words to best paint a picture of just how dreadful it is not only to be in prison at Christmas, but also to be in severe pain. We say our goodbyes, and I return to my cold cell where I stay for the rest of the day.

About 7.00pm, the pain has become a lot worse, I consider pressing the emergency button to the left of the light switch and asking for an ambulance to be called. I am convinced that three days of this severe pain in my head is something more sinister than a migraine, perhaps I've developed a tumor. Instead I jam a pair of earplugs in to drown out the ghetto-blasting neighbours enjoying what they can of Christmas, and disappear beneath the duvet in the hope that my body will find some way of healing itself.

Sunday 27th December

Wake at 8.30am. The pain isn't as severe, but still lingers. I take it very easy today. 2.30pm, I'm feeling much better, enough to chat with Nafir and Delroy. I make my usual appointment to phone Jess before returning to my cell to waste the day away by watching TV. Lights out 10.00pm.

Monday 28th Dec.

I've had a decent night's sleep, the first in a while. I spend the day replying to the people who've kindly sent Christmas cards. I find myself duplicating the same sentence in each letter of reply, if I had my lap top I would simply copy and paste. I try to remain upbeat in my letters, but very little has happened and once I've written the first paragraph I still have thirty-three blank lines to fill on my A4 sheet of writing paper.

My new position as HOPIN rep (Helping Other Prisoners In Need) is put to use when I'm asked to write a letter to an inmate's solicitor regarding his visitation rights to his seven-year old son. He shows me a file of paperwork which contains very private and sensitive information about his case. I can't resist the offer to read the file, but its content has left me with a sick feeling in the pit of my stomach. It isn't fair of me to share this detail with you, but let's say there is no way this man should be allowed anywhere near his son, or any other child, ever. I write the letter and leave.

Next is a twenty nine year old Asian guy called Raj, sentenced to nine years for two Section 18 assaults. He wants advice on how to deal with a complaint against an officer. He recently arrived on this wing from A wing where he was a victim of having excrement smeared into his clothes and bed linen. He tells me that this has happened several times when he has left his single cell. He was moved off the wing when he threatened the officer he believed to be responsible. He tells me that it has started all over again, and this time he suspects officer Phoenix. I advise him to take the appropriate grievance procedure, the last thing he should consider is attacking the officer. He only has eight weeks left of his sentence. Officer Phoenix is sitting twenty yards away joking and laughing with another officer which upsets Raj. I calm him down and we write a statement detailing his grievance.

Tuesday 29th Dec

Back to class to complete the course work with Hilary who signs off our individual files. She asks each of us to complete a questionnaire to give a general overview of how effective the course has been. This prompts me to reflect on the past six weeks and the journey I've been on. I met a group of people who I have got to know relatively well, there have been clashes of personality and constant competition to be the alpha male within the group, but overall they have been a good bunch of lads. I will particularly miss the company of Geordie who has a great sense of humour, and enjoys clever banter.

After lunch the course is brought to an end. Hilary has brought in a selection box of chocolate biscuits which are shared around as we play giant dominos in teams. A pleasant afternoon, and an excellent end to Hilary's course.

During evening association my phone call to Jess is interrupted by Ben who is looking flushed and is sporting a huge grin on his face. When I ask what he's up to, he leans forward and breathes in my face. I can detect the faint aroma of alcohol. He invites me to follow him to the end of the wing, to a cupboard containing mops, buckets, brooms and cleaning fluids. The cupboard is very warm as many of the pipes that feed the wing's radiator originate here. There is a pungent smell which at first I assumed is the cleaning products. However, I am shown two, one gallon containers of a liquid, I am told that this is Hooch. It is made of three ingredients; juice, yeast and sugar. I am offered a cup, but am concerned about the whole Hooch making process and decline the kind offer. I am reliably informed that this homemade grog packs a punch and I am missing out. This is confirmed by those who've had a scoop or two and are staggering around the wing giggling like pathetic little school girls, drunk as the proverbial skunk. It is fun to watch.

Wednesday 30th Dec.

Arriving in the classroom one by one come the revelers of last night with a hangover from hell. Hooch has done its job. Needless to say the morning session is a very quiet affair.

This evening the first post since Christmas is delivered. A few late Christmas cards, a letter from colleague Michael Collie, and one from my boss Chas Watkin who was responsible for giving me the job at *Midlands Today* and has consistently supported me throughout my time at the BBC.

Thursday 31st Dec, New Year's Eve.

Play a game of scrabble in class. It becomes heated when a fellow inmate tries to claim points for the word *EVA*. When I point out that it has to be a word rather than a person's name he stares at me with a puzzled expression. He argues that it isn't a name it is indeed a word. To settle the disagreement I ask him to give me a sentence with the word *eva* in it. He agrees and begins his sentence thus;

"You can *eva* choose to give me the points or get a smack in the mouth".

I look for the slightest hint of humour in his expression, but he is deadly serious. Now, he is much bigger than me, so I have a choice, I could *eva* point out his mistake and correct him, or just let him have the points.

11.45am marks the end of this course, and this particular part of my prison journey. It has been eventful to say the least. The course has taught me something about people, well, men in prison anyway.

After lunch I am taken to the visits block for a visit from Jess. While waiting in the holding room Dez, a race relations representative on C-Wing, informs me that quite a number of complaints have been submitted by inmates objecting to me being transferred to G-Wing. They have sited *favouritism* as their main grievance, and believe I'm being fast tracked through the system.

It is so good to see Jess. After ten minutes we've run out of things to tell each other about the past week, so we settle for small talk, nevertheless it is just so nice to be in her company. 4.00pm and time to say goodbye once again, the same familiar feeling, I hate goodbyes.

As the hall is cleared of visitors I am *randomly* picked out and beckoned by a young male officer of about twenty-five years old to enter a small room. I am told to stand on four grey carpet tiles. There is an elderly officer of about sixty-years. I have a vague idea of what is about to happen, but I can't understand why I have been chosen. The young officer explains that a strip search is about to take place and asks whether I have something on me that I shouldn't. The answer is, "of course not". He tells me to remove all of my clothing which I do. I stand there, starkers, as the young officer scrutinizes my naked flesh for anything I may have been trying to smuggle into his fortress. Needless to say I've concealed nothing in or about my person, the whole procedure is extremely embarrassing, degrading and achieves nothing, but to give the young officer a great story to tell his pals down the pub for years to come.

5.30, it's early association. I guess officers have New Year's parties to attend. I speak to Jess for the last time this year, take a shower and am banged up.

I reflect, as one does at this time, over the past year, what an ordeal. This time last year Jess and I were transforming our relatively successful restaurant into the Wild West with bales of hay and blow-up cacti, the theme for our New Year's celebrations. Little did I know then what the New Year would have in store for me. If anyone would have told me, I'd have thought they'd be a worthy patient for a mental asylum.

So, here I am, one year on, in a very different place both physically and mentally.

I watch TV until around 11.30pm. I push my earplugs firmly into my ears, and try to fall asleep before the turn of the New Year. However, I am jolted out of my semi-comatose state when the wing erupts, doors are banged, shouts, whistles and singing.

Beyond the prison walls fireworks light up the night sky. Here it is, a new year, a new decade. The racket continues for around twenty minutes, I drift off to sleep.

Friday 1st Jan 2010.

I wake up at 7.24am. The New Year has brought with it a new, positive mood for me. Thought of the day: In dark times light always get through, hope will always defeat fear.

I wait until the afternoon to phone Jess. She's been with her sister to see in the New Year. I wish her a happy 2010, and we looked forward to being together again. Next on my call list is my son Calam. Disappointment again as his phone goes straight to voicemail. I call my sister Abi who is very pleased to hear from me. I am in a very sociable mood today and spend time speaking to lots of fellow inmates on association.

4.30pm dinner, chicken curry with rice then bang-up. Watched TV until 1.00am and that is it, I've survived Christmas and New Year in prison, time to move on.

Saturday 2nd Jan 2010.

Awake at 8.15am, sit watching Saturday morning TV. 10.30am association, which I decline, preferring instead to remain in my cell to watch *Saturday Morning Kitchen* with James Martin, a favourite TV programme of mine and a reminder of what food should taste like. Despite preferring to remain in the relative peace of my cell I am paid a window visit first by Nafir followed fifteen minutes later by Delroy. Both classmates have only five weeks left of their sentence, and both are becoming increasingly strange in their behaviour. I learn it's a common trait for career prisoners, it's called being *Gate Happy*, and is best defined as the anticipation of being released causing anxiety coupled with euphoria, the two emotions battle against each other and produce this weird behaviour in the individual. By way of an early celebration Delroy invites me to a drinks party as the next batch of Hooch will be ready on Monday which also coincides with the brewer's birthday.

2.30pm, association, shower, phone Jess, who suggests she speaks to a PR agency with regard to managing press interest upon my release.

Decide to stay out on association and play my first game of pool for ages on a small rickety table, the type you'd find in a kids bedroom. I share one pool cue with a Chinese guy. My playing pool attracts the attention of a small crowd of "experts", Delroy Smithen being one of them, all keen to point out my bad technique. This is gold dust to Delroy who's been looking for something to criticize me on for a while. I leave the table having lost, blaming far too much interest in my game. I'm not a competitive person, I prefer to play for recreation, however, I'm reminded just what a competitive environment I'm in. I'll be very reluctant to play again.

I spend the rest of the evening watching TV and reading, boredom is really setting in. Lights out 10.30pm.

Sunday 3rd Jan 2010.

8.15am I decide to have breakfast today, sausage, fried egg, spaghetti hoops. I choose not to participate in the first association, opting instead to write letters to former colleagues who sent beautiful Christmas cards containing even more beautiful thoughts and wishes.

Lunch today is roast chicken-leg, mash, and sprouts, treacle roly-poly and custard for dessert. I have managed to acquire a tin opener from a neighbouring inmate who in return needs a prison issue pillow, a fair swap I reckon, I can now open my can of tuna and can of pineapple chunks which have been sitting here for a couple of weeks.

2.30pm, association. I spend half an hour on the phone to Jess who is feeling very down and needs cheering up. I try as best I can, but nothing is better than a big hug when someone's feeling down, and I am very aware I am unable to do that, which, in turn upsets and frustrates me. Jess and I are a great team, we're crap when we're apart, she's my soul-mate, my right arm and I really feel for her. When she hurts, I hurt and the feeling of not being able to comfort her is unbelievable, it's torture. After talking to Jess I want to return to my cell and hide from the world inside jail, but I'll just mope, so I decide to stay out on association where I am invited to play a game of pool. After scanning the area *Mr.*

Envious (Delroy Smithen) is nowhere to be seen, so I accept. Win one, lose one, but as the third game starts Smithen appears, scrutinizing my every shot, he just can't let me play a simple game of pool without turning it into a coaching session.

4.30pm, dinner and bang up. I spend the evening writing and returning my colourful Christmas grotto of a cell to its dreary, former, depressing state. Lights out midnight.

Monday 4th Jan 2010

Wake at 8.00am and get myself ready, but there is no class for me today as I've completed the course and I'm still waiting to hear whether I have a new job as the chapel orderly. The morning is spent locked up watching TV, every minute drags.

The afternoon is much the same, although I was paid a window visit from Delroy Smithen who asks me to buy him some tobacco as his canteen order has been messed up. I don't particularly want to help him out as he has been nothing but a pain in the ass to me and he now wants my help. Despite this I agree that he is welcome to any surplus cash I have once I have made my purchases.

6.00pm unlocked and taken to reception to pick up several parcels that have arrived at the prison during the Christmas period. A Christmas stocking crammed full with all sorts of goodies from the Ash family, Nicola, Richard, Olivia, Imogen and William, friends of mine from Sutton Coldfield. What a lovely thing to do. I'm not allowed to keep the contents of my stocking, prison rules don't allow it, so the stocking will be put with my personal belongings until I'm released. Another parcel contains Chris Evan's autobiography, a Christmas present from Jess. I'm so grateful.

The evening is spent reading and watching TV. Lights out at midnight with this thought of the day in my head;

"It's not what you've got in your life, it's who you've got".

And that makes me a very lucky man.

Tuesday 5th Jan 2010.

I wake at 8.15am. I'm still unemployed, but nevertheless I get myself ready just in case a last minute vacancy becomes available, I'll be good to go. 8.45am, my door is unlocked by Officer Chadwick just to confirm that I am indeed still unemployed before locking the door again. I get back into bed fully clothed as the cell is at around zero degrees with the insecure window allowing a wind chill. From beneath my duvet I waste the day away by reading and watching TV.

6.30pm association breaks the boredom. I phone my best pal Gez who's off to Moscow next week for his latest adventure abroad to try to make his millions. It is great to talk to him and hear what he's been up to over the Christmas period. He confirms I haven't missed anything, and due to my circumstances it is a Christmas he chooses to forget. I am the nucleus of our circle of friends, with me out of the picture he says it seems everyone has put their social life on hold, and rarely does the group come together. We further chat about his ambition to make it big in the financial sector in Russia, and as always I wish him every success. I agree to call him again before he leaves our shores, and needless to say I will miss him hugely.

On the way to the shower I stop to chat with Senior Officer Lewis, Officer Phoenix and Officer Morgan. It is the most normal conversation I've had since being inside. Miss Lewis and Mr. Phoenix both have twenty years of service, and I'm interested to know how prison has changed during their time. They are more than happy to share their experiences with me, and the chat gives me the opportunity to get a steer on Officer Phoenix, who you may recall I was told had taken a dislike to me. It turns out that he does not have a problem with me, and we seem to get on very well.

After taking a shower Officer Phoenix is keen to continue our conversation this time it is just myself and him. He talks about my case and it is his belief that I was stitched up. He sympathizes with my situation and recalls a similar incident he'd been in himself which could have easily gone the wrong way. It is reassuring to hear Mr. Phoenix talk like this, and I get the impression he is a decent bloke. I believe whatever opinion he had of me before our chat has changed also.

281

7.30pm back to cell for bang-up, lights out 11.00pm

Wednesday 6th Jan.

Wake at 8.00am. I don't bother getting ready as if for work, no point, although I do feel guilty. It's part of my work ethic to want to work rather than lay around all day doing nothing. In a three by twelve foot cell, however, there really isn't anything to do, so I stay in bed for as long as possible. The news is reporting the longest cold snap in thirty years, the UK is losing 1.4 billion pounds a day as the work force is unable to get to work. Beneath my duvet seems to be the best place to be today.

I spend the time reading, watching TV and carrying out some cell exercises to keep warm.

11.45am lunch is served. I have a chat with Dean, the classroom assistant and neighbour, he's been talking to Neil who runs a gym course and Neil has been asking about whether I'd like to join the course. Sounds great so I complete an application. I have lost count of the amount of applications I have completed and am still awaiting a result for. An app' for a kitchen job, Chapel job, a Listeners job, app' for HEP B injections, and an app' to see the dentist.

2.30pm my door is unlocked by Miss Aston to announce that I start work in the kitchen at 8.45am tomorrow, some good news. Work in the kitchen is only carried out by inmates who are most trusted for obvious reasons, preparing food using knives. It is one of the best paid jobs in the prison and carries with it several privileges. It means from tomorrow I won't be banged up all day. Kitchen work is referred to as a *bird-killer*, not that anyone is required to kill any birds you understand. Bird is a slang word for doing time. The kitchen is always a hive of activity, preparing as many as seven hundred and sixty meals twice a day. It's hard work, and employees are always on the go seven days a week meaning time flies by, hence the term *bird-killer*. I'm looking forward to my new role and working my way to head chef before long.

Thursday 7th Jan 2010.

Wake at 7.45am. Get ready to start my first day at my new job. 8.45am I arrive at the prison kitchens. I am given a set of chef whites and given my first responsibility, "tea-packs". A tea-pack is given to every prisoner at lunch time each day. It is my job to prepare these tea-packs. I put four teabags, five sachets of sugar and five sachets of whitener into a small cellophane bag sealing it closed with a simple taping machine. I'm part of a three man production line and we need to complete at least seven hundred and fifty packs per day. My new colleagues are Dale from Walsall, in for stealing wooden pallets, and Darren from Stechford in Birmingham, nicked for stealing a safe from a school. We make a good team and during the morning complete more than the minimum requirement for the entire day.

10.30am tea break where I enjoy two pieces of wholemeal toast with marmalade, the first I've tasted for over four months and it tastes delicious. I'm going to like working in the kitchen.

11.45am back to the wing for lunch where I witness my morning's work of packing tea-packs being handed out to inmates. I'm sure the novelty will soon wear off.

1.30pm I'm taken to the visit block. Jess looks great and we chat and hold hands the entire visit. Gutted to see her leave, but I'm getting used to the familiar emotions, although it never gets any easier to deal with.

Lights out at 11.15pm after a busy day, I am ready for a good night's sleep.

Friday 8th Jan 2010.

Report to the kitchens for my second day on the new job at 8.45am. After an hour of producing tea-packs, I, along with four other new employees, am taken to a classroom to begin our induction. We watch a DVD about food hygiene which is presented by a former TV colleague, Phillipa Forrester, and Tony Robinson who I'd beaten to become Best TV Personality of the Year in 2002 at the *Royal Television Society Awards*.

Then the class is asked to complete a simple test about food hygiene.

After lunch back to bagging more tea-packs which is already becoming very monotonous.

4.15pm, seven hundred and sixty meals have been prepared and are being collected by workers from the various prison wings. As we're leaving the kitchen each worker is handed a carton of a half a pint of fresh milk, another privilege of working in the kitchen. A small but very much appreciated gift.

Back in my cell, canteen has been delivered along with a letter from my former boss at BBC *Watchdog*, now the Editor of BBC's *The One Show*, Doug Carnegie. He is very supportive with his words and urges me to keep my chin up.

Saturday 9th Jan 2010.

Off to work at 9.00am, it is great to have something to do at the weekend for a change and this new role is living up to its nickname of *bird-killer*. I'm working alone packing tea-packs today, but despite this I complete more than the minimum required.

During lunch Dave Young-Smith, my former pad mate, has become the newest resident on D Wing. It's good to see him and I show him around the wing and introduce him to the movers and shakers. He takes the cell directly opposite me.

During afternoon association I keep my regular appointment to call Jess who is safe and sound. I spend the afternoon writing letters and watching TV. Lights out at midnight.

Sunday 10th Jan 2010.

Manage to pack five hundred tea-packs before lunch meaning I am well ahead for the next few days, and means I'm not required for an afternoon shift. Lunch today is a very tasty chicken curry with pitta bread.

1.45pm association, I speak to Jess who is a little worse for wear with a hangover having spent a night out with the girls. Needless to say the conversation is brief, but worth hearing her voice.
Monday 11th Jan 2010.

In the kitchen by 8.30am more tea-pack packing.

Tuesday 12th Jan 2010.

My role in the kitchen is becoming very tedious. I'm keen to move on from packing tea packs and wonder whether my cooking skills will ever be required.

During lunch I am asked to complete some paperwork for my assessment for Home Detention Curfew which is due on April 20th. I am surprised, but very pleased that the process of considering me for HDC has begun so early. The file consists of various sections assessing my suitability for release on tag. I'm happy to read a section entitled Prison Staff Member Report. It reads:

Ashley has been on D Wing for two months, in that time he has been polite and respectful to staff at all times, he is no control problem, he complies with prison and wing rules.

It is completed by Officer Stacy. Another section asks for details of where I propose to live and what I intend to do to occupy my time while I'm on HDC. I complete the sections and write about my intention to produce a TV programme called *Behind The 9's* during this time. I am happy with the completed forms, all sections are favourable, and therefore there should be no delay in me being released at the earliest opportunity I believe.

1.45pm visit time. It is great to see Jess, but I can tell immediately there is something on her mind. It takes a while but I manage to coax it out of her. She has concerns about my relationship with a female colleague and friend from work. I explain what our relationship was, and try to convince Jess that there is nothing more to it. I reassure Jess about our future, the visit is a good clearing of the air.

Wednesday 13th Jan 2010.

Tea-packs, five hundred flaming tea-packs, lights out 11.00pm

Thursday 14th Jan 2010.

8.45am back to the tea-packs. Just when I think I can't take the monotony anymore I'm told by an officer that I have been selected onto the part-time gym course which starts on Monday morning. So my day will now consist of mornings in the gym, afternoons in the kitchen, perfect, the best of both worlds, this is going very well, I think.

Friday 15th Jan 2010.

I am working alone today, but happily complete seven hundred tea-packs in my own little world, until I am joined by a chap called Lenny. Lenny is a Hell's Angel. He has been sentenced to six years for fighting at Birmingham International Airport in 2008, one of the stories I'd reported on. Lenny has been a Hell's Angel for nine years. He's around fifty-five years of age, bald, stands about five foot six, with a strong Black Country accent. He has the words *Hell's Angel* tattooed on his back in thick set letters across his shoulders. He's very pleasant, and talks fondly of his membership of the group. I express great interest and suggest we produce a documentary about the Hell's Angels. He likes the idea and is keen to dispel many of the myths of the much feared group.

Saturday 16th Jan 2010.

Morning shift in the kitchen, but I have the afternoon off, so happily crack on with *the* most boring job in the kitchen, tea-packs!

Sunday 17th Jan 2010.

Among the six items of post to arrive today, I was pleased to receive a letter from my good friend and colleague Lindsay Doyle, from BBC Midlands Today. Despite her plum BBC accent, Lindsay is actually a scouser. She's a truly fabulous, versatile reporter, able to turn her hand to all matter of news subject, and has a great story about how her cat *Bibi* once saved her from carbon monoxide poisoning. Lindsay writes with good news about how she has been awarded the position of Arts & Culture Reporter, a position I had for many years until I was dismissed. The job couldn't have gone to a better person, and it's one of the better decisions BBC management have made. Well done Linds.

Monday 18th Jan 2010.

7.50am, get myself together, ready for a new week behind bars. Report to the gym at 8.45am to be told that I'm not on the list and the gym is full today, I'll have to return to my wing. As I am about to leave another officer calls me back, writes my name at the bottom of a typed list of names and tells me to go in.

I am directed to a classroom in which are sat ten other inmates. I am given a literacy test to complete, and answer all fifty-eight questions. The paper is marked, my score is 58 out of 58. After an hour in the classroom we are allowed to change into prison issue shorts and vest top to use the gym facilities.

Start with the treadmill, two kilometers in twelve minutes. Then play a game of soft tennis, it feels good to be exercising.

After lunch it is back to the kitchen to produce more tea-packs, but this time I feel energized.

Tuesday 19th Jan 2010.

In the classroom at the gym I am given another test, Level Two Literacy this time, again fifty-eight questions, with the same result.

In the gym I'm approached by a guy called Tristan Dooley, a personal trainer on the outside who kindly agrees to become my personal trainer on the inside. As he puts me through my paces, it seems to me that he knows what he's doing and it's not long before I feel the pain of his knowledge throughout my entire body.

11.45am break for lunch, during which I'm told to pack up my cell as I'm moving to the 4's. I spend the next hour packing away the accumulated mass I've accrued in my tiny cell. I'm amazed just how much stuff I've managed to hoard.

1.45pm my door is unlocked and I'm told I have just ten minutes to move cells during the *route*. The route is when the whole prison is on the move after being banged up. This happens whenever inmates have to move en masse to attend work. To move cells is going to take at least twenty minutes as I have to make several trips single handedly carrying my stuff up three flights of stairs.

My new cell is exactly the same layout but at least twice the size. It's clean and better equipped, with more shelves and cupboards, and being on the top landing it is so much warmer than my cell in the basement. One wall is completely covered with A4 size posters of naked women welcoming me to my new abode. As beautiful as they are, why torture myself with such images, they have to go, but maybe not just yet.

I throw my belongings into the cell to sort out later and head off to work in the kitchen. Another welcome sight is three new tea packers. I am no longer the new kid in the kitchen and no longer a one man production line. The role of tea packing is now over-staffed which allows me to take a supervisory role.

3.30pm I am taken to reception to pick up a parcel. It is a new quilt cover and hair cutting clippers I'd ordered before Christmas. Great, today is like Christmas, new cell, new presents.

As I get back to my new home, waiting outside is a brand new mattress, another prezzie for me to unwrap. Simple things, but how important they've become. Under the glare of a bevy of butt naked beauties on my wall I set about arranging my new home with a smile on my face and the first feeling of mild contentment I've experienced for months.

During association I telephone Jess to tell her about my move and to catch up with all that is happening in the outside world. 11.30pm lights out, I settle down for what I'm sure will be a great night's sleep.

Wednesday 20th Jan 2010.

Wake at 7.24am after a very restless night, a combination of my newly discovered muscles hurting, unfamiliar surroundings, and my new cell is totally tropical compared to what I've been used to.

Waking up early has the benefit of owning your day rather than chasing it. As lovely as they are, my one night stand with the fifteen beauties on the wall, left by the previous occupant, is over and they have to go. I carefully prize them off the wall so as not to tear them, perhaps another inmate will have a *use* for them.

8.45am I head off to the gym for an hour of classroom, another literacy test, then an hour with my personal trainer, Tristan, who barks orders at his new pupil, he takes his job very seriously, and I respect our trainer pupil relationship.

While taking a shower I hear my name being shouted;

"BLAKE, there's an officer here to see you."

I dry and change as quickly as possible. As I come out of the changing room I am greeted by Mr. Hancock who tells me to pack up my cell during lunch time as I am moving to G Wing this afternoon;

"That's if you're still interested!" he says.

"Absolutely" I reply enthusiastically shaking his hand.

I am over the moon but keep the news to myself to avoid any jealousy.

During lunch I excitedly pack up all the stuff I'd just unpacked. When I've finished I have two neat piles of my belongings ready to go. I've calculated it will only take me two trips. I sit on the end of my bed awaiting the arrival of Mr. Hancock.

1.45pm my door is unlocked to attend work. As I won't be going to work this afternoon I wait in my cell doorway and watch others leaving the wing in their usual loud, boyish way. Nafir sees me standing there and is intrigued as to why I'm not going anywhere. He comes over and catches sight of my two neat piles at the end of my bed. He thinks I've been released from prison until I explain that I am off to G Wing imminently which is met by shock and disappointment. He seems genuinely upset to hear I am leaving D Wing. We say our goodbyes, and I thank him for looking after me during my time on here, I wish him luck upon his release in a few weeks, and with that we are locked behind our doors again.

2.45pm I hear the jangle of keys approaching my door, with a clunky turn of the lock the door is flung open, it is Mr. Hancock who has brought with him two Asian lads to give me a hand with my stuff. This is what I've been waiting for, for so long, I'm finally going to G Wing. What follows is like checking out of a hotel, the two lads being the bell boys, it isn't what I expected. As I am leaving the wing I say goodbye to Elliot, and thank him for making me feel welcome and safe, also to Paul Wright (Wrighty), again for being so good to me and doing a great job cutting my hair. I leave D Wing to walk a short distance to the exclusive G Wing.

G Wing

As I arrive, G wing is deadly quiet. It has the feel of an old people's nursing home, a clean, modern building with soft chairs and curtains on the double glazed windows, a stark contrast to what I've experienced of jail so far. My belongings are taken up a small flight of stairs and along a long corridor. The corridor looks more like a typical prison with standard thick metal prison doors either side. Once I enter G2-10 the cell more resembles a room at a Travel Lodge hotel. There are tea and coffee making facilities, a TV with remote control, and a self-controlled radiator. The en-suite, yes en-suite, features a white ceramic toilet with drop down toilet seat, a wash basin and a shower. Wow, my own shower to have whenever I please! The cell even has a key-lockable safe cupboard. This is why everyone wants to live on G Wing, it's everything I'd heard about, it doesn't feel like prison anymore, this is luxury by comparison.

Mr. Hancock shows me around. During the tour the rules of G Wing are told to me and I am required to sign a form, a contractual agreement to accept the terms and conditions of my residency.

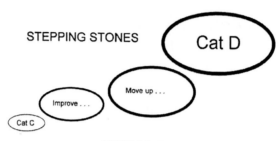

G WING COMPACT

G wing is a new accommodation which has superior facilities and as such you are in a privileged position having been selected for the Stepping Stones project.

The following are instances which would result in your removal from G wing. Please note this is not an exhaustive list and a wing Board can be convened at any time to evaluate the suitability of a prisoner for G wing:

- failure to show respect to all member of staff and visitors;
- failure to treat each other with respect and decency at all times showing no prejudice towards each other;
- refusal to attend identified programmes, activities and work or being removed from such;
- losing your enhanced status;
- being classified as a communal cell by the doctor;
- being on an open ACCT document;
- failing to maintain a level of behaviour expected from an enhanced prisoner;
- refusing or failing any drug test;
- failing to maintain an acceptable standard of hygiene/cleanliness;
- failure to adhere to or comply with any of the establishment's policies, examples being – race relations, discrimination, diversity, equal opportunities, decency, smoking;
- if you are subject to the establishment's anti-social behaviour policy (anti-bullying);
- being in the area behind the wing (by outside wall) unescorted.

I have read and agree to the terms and conditions of this Compact and have been given a copy to keep in my possession.

Witnessed by:

Prisoner's name ...... BLAKE ......   Name ...... A. Hancock ......

Prisoner's number ...... A2043AM ......   Rank ...... Officer ......

Prisoner's signature ....   Signature ....

Date ...... 26.01.10 ......   Date ...... 26.01.10 ......

This declaration must be placed in the prisoner's wing file

I am even taken on a tour of the private gardens which are landscaped and kept in pristine condition by G Wing residents. There is a Zen Garden complete with four foot high, gold Buddha beside two ponds and a water feature, very Feng Shui. Turns out this is right below my window.

G Wing is fabulous and is run completely differently to what I've experienced so far. In hindsight, I guess I'm pleased to have experienced the levels of accommodation that I have so far otherwise I couldn't appreciate what I have now so much.

Mr. Hancock leaves me to unpack and settle in. It doesn't take long for word to get around that I am now in residence, and a small welcome committee arrive at my door to politely introduce themselves, no doubt to meet the fallen star from the telly.

My afternoon is spent getting to know how things work on G Wing, there is a steady stream of curious visitors to my cell/room.

When I phone Jess she instantly notices the background is very quiet, I break the news that I've moved to G Wing, and she is delighted. She can now worry less about me.

The evening is spent getting used to my new surroundings. Lights out at around 11.30pm with a strange feeling of a smile on my face, strange because a smile is something of a rarity around these parts.

Thursday 21st Jan 2010

Awake at 7.55am after a good night's sleep. The wing is eerily quiet compared to my last place and it takes some getting used to.

Spend the morning at the gym. I use the treadmill and weights. After, a math's test in the classroom.

After lunch I prepare for my visit from Jess. It is a pleasure to shower in the privacy of my own bathroom and to shave in a proper sink with a mirror which has been purposefully mounted onto the wall, rather than a mirror tile stuck on with toothpaste. I shall refer to my cell as a room from now on, as the word cell revokes images of a dark, damp and dingy hell-hole, that would give you the wrong impression, this is far from it.

1.30pm I'm collected from my room and taken to the visits block. It takes until 2.45pm to see Jess. The new visiting system introduced a few days ago, which is meant to speed the process up, isn't working. Nevertheless it is great to see my girl who is full of good news about our new home, and that my probation officer has been in touch to arrange to visit the house as part of the preparation for my release on Home Detention Curfew on April 20th. It is good to hear things are progressing without a hitch. The rest of the time we spend enjoying each other's company before the visit is over all too quickly. Long goodbyes of kissing and hugging, neither of us wanting to let go, both of us battling to stay strong in each other's presence. Again I keep my eyes fixed on her as she makes her way out of the visiting hall, she constantly glances back to cram in a few final images of me before she disappears through the door and out of sight for another week. My heart sinks to the bottom of my chest, tears are desperately trying to overflow my eye lids like a flooded river about to burst its banks, I use all my effort to dam the flow.

As we're waiting for the visits room to empty of visitors a young officer invites me into the room I now know is where I get strip searched. I assume the position on the four square carpet tiles in the centre of the small room as I'm told I'm about to be searched. I'm asked to remove my sweatshirt, then my shirt, my jeans, shoes and socks, finally my underwear. The strip takes place during a conversation between the two officers and me as to whether I'm ever to return to reading the news. It is most bizarre. During the naked conversation we talk about my colleague and good friend Nick Owen. Believe me when I tell you, this is the first time I have spoken about Nick Owen whilst being naked. I try to pay no attention to what is happening to me, and carry on as though I am unfazed, partly because it is unbelievable, and partly because I don't want to give the officers the satisfaction of thinking they are humiliating me in anyway. If they enjoy looking at my form then who am I to deny them their desire, it's not as if I have anything to hide. I re-dress and leave the two young officers with a story they'll no doubt be sharing with their pals down the pub tonight.

During this evening's association I decide to socialize in a communal room which has a large TV, a table tennis table, pool table, dart board, a bookcase full of reading material, and soft comfy chairs. The room reminds me of a school staff room. I meet and chat to my new neighbours who are all very pleasant, a complete contrast to my previous experiences of association. 7.45pm it's time for bang-up, which just seems to happen without any drama as does usually happen when trying to get cons behind their doors. I'm convinced that in the unlikely event that a G Wing inmate didn't want to bang-up, an officer would politely invite him to 'take occupancy of one's abode', such is the contrast here. Lights out 11.30pm.

Friday 22nd Jan 2010.

Wake at 6.55am. Off to the gym classroom at 8.30am. After an hour of math's testing I am able to use the gym with Tristan as my trainer. Today he wants me to concentrate on arms and chest. Apart from the pain, I'm already beginning to feel the improvements.

After lunch I am introduced to my new job. Being a resident of G Wing means I am unable to be employed in the kitchen anymore, therefore I'm given a new job in the prison stores room, another highly trusted position. As part of my new role at 3.00pm every Friday I'm asked, along with three other colleagues, to collect four trollies of dirty laundry from E & F Wings. These wings house Vulnerable Prisoners who are kept separate from the main stream of prisoners for fear of attack. We take these trollies to the laundry department and drop them off, the whole job takes twenty minutes.

The evening is spent writing and watching TV. I make a point of watching the 10.25pm edition of BBC *Midlands Today* which is presented by Michael Collie. It is exactly a year ago to the day that I sat where he is and presented my last news bulletin, little did I know at the time how life was to change. Lights out 11.30pm.

Saturday 23rd Jan 2010.

Wake at 8.30am, what a difference G Wing is at the weekend compared to C & D Wings, its quiet and relaxed. I spend much of the day writing letters.

Sunday 24th January 2010 (my son Calam's birthday).

Wake at 8.30am. Shortly after my door is unlocked I am visited by a chap called Jeff who comes bearing gifts. He has a pair of green curtains he thinks I might like, I accept his kind and thoughtful gesture. Next I receive a visit from Hussain who asks me if I'd like a game of chess. I decline for two reasons, firstly I don't know how to play chess, and secondly I want to watch *The Big Question*, with Nicky Campbell, the programme is debating the right of self-defence.

After lunch I get to know more of my fellow wing mates by playing table tennis and pool. The evening is spent writing and thinking about my son Calam. It's his twentieth birthday today, and I can't be with him. It is also a year ago today that this whole nightmare began.
Lights out 10.30pm.

Monday 25th Jan 2010.

Usual morning session in the gym being trained by Tristan. The afternoon sees the start of my new job in C.E.S. Central

Equipment Stores. I'm working with Taff another G Wing resident. Taff is the Hell's Angel who equipped me with various items when I first arrived at HMP Stafford. He takes me through what's required. Between us we're responsible for stocking seven wings with their required kit, from boots to pyjamas. My first afternoon is straight forward enough, though physically demanding; stacking, lifting, carrying, dragging. Along with my sessions in the gym, this job will help keep me fit and ensure a good night's sleep.

4.00pm back to the wing for dinner and association.

7.00pm speak to Jess who is upbeat and happy as she's been offered a job with energy drinks maker *Red Bull*. Lights out 11.00pm.

Tuesday 26th Jan 2010.

After the best night's sleep I've had for months I wake late at 8.20am. Off to the gym at 8.45am to spend an hour in the classroom completing another literacy test before Tristan trains me.

Afternoon is spent at my new job.

Wednesday 27th Jan 2010.

Wake at 7.50am, door is unlocked at 8.20am when I immediately phone Jess to wish her well for her first day at her new *Red Bull* job.

Gym in the morning, store-room work in the afternoon.

During evening association several wing mates pay me a visit to chat. I am fascinated as they are happy to tell me about their crimes; a rape, a murder dropped to manslaughter, and a young drug dealer. Their stories are interesting, saddening, and some are sickening.

Thursday 28th Jan 2010.

Spend the first hour in the classroom learning fractions, not my strongest subject. Then into the gym for more personal training with Tristan.

After lunch, work at the stores. Today I'm working with Taff and Scouse who are both competing to be top dog, the alpha male in the store room. I'm forced to hold my own in the banter stakes otherwise it will be determined that I'm the weakest link. It is interesting to watch the psychology.

There is no association this evening, but I do manage to speak to Jess briefly before being banged up.

Friday 29th Jan 2010.

Unlocked at 8.20am and am told to report to the office immediately. Waiting there is Mr. Wareham from the Offenders Management Unit. He has a copy of my updated prison file which we go through and sign. My new score is low, meaning I'm considered to be a low risk level. I take the opportunity to ask about the likelihood of being granted early release on Home detention Curfew, and I am disappointed with his response. He says it is unlikely that I'll be granted HDC due to the nature of my offence, but says he will check it out. This news leaves me feeling down. Jess is relying on me coming home in April, suddenly it looks unlikely. How am I going to break this bad news to her? The rest of the morning I spend trying to deal with this disappointment, I decide to look on the bright side, at least I'm on G Wing with all its comfort, if I have to be here until the end of my sentence then I guess I'll just have to cope somehow, Jess is a different story however. I get to thinking maybe it's better that she moves on from me. She has started a new job, she'll meet new people, she's moving forward and I'm holding her back. All these thoughts are rushing through my head and there's little I can do to stop them. Another thing Mr. Wareham informed me of during our meeting this morning is that I would have usually gone straight to a Category D, Open prison, but because of the media interest it is political that I am seen to be doing my sentence, hence why I ended up here at HMP Stafford. Again my status as a minor celeb' seems to be working against me.

Saturday 30th Jan 2010.

I wake at 7.48am to a cloudless, bright, crisp, winter's sky. It is glorious. Yesterday's meeting is playing on my mind. Jess is visiting later and I search for ways to tell her the disappointing news, it's only fair that she prepares for the worst. Is it right to ask her to wait for me until September, or is it best to let her go and get on with her new life? I know what she'll say, but what will happen in reality? These thoughts are making me very anxious and depressed, I feel really sorry for myself and just want to curl up and cry myself to sleep. I need to pull myself out of this state before Jess arrives.

1.30pm I'm collected to make the short journey across to the visits block where Jess is waiting. Jess has the ability to make everything instantly feel much better. She excitedly tells me about her new job and new adventures. After about forty-five minutes I pluck up the courage to tell her about my concerns that I could be refused early release. Meaning I'll be here until 1st September, eight months away. Jess immediately assures me that if this is to happen then she'll remain faithfully here throughout, and has no desire to move on. She explains that she has cried with anger and frustration that this is happening to us, it's not as if I brought it on myself, and that it could happen to anyone. Her words pick me up from the deep depression I've been in. To hear her say them empowers me with a new strength to carry on and get through this nightmare. I feel extremely lucky to have Jess with me throughout this ordeal, my best friend and future wife, I'm a very lucky man.

Sunday 31st Jan 2010.

I spend the morning in my room writing letters. I am happy to keep myself to myself, however, I receive visits from several inmates who want to find out more about me. I politely answer their questions which include what famous people I've interviewed, politics, and my views on the justice system.

On the way back to my room, after posting my letters, I am invited into a neighboring room for a cup of tea with Banksy (drug dealer) Scouse (armed robbery) and Nathan (death by dangerous driving). The conversation is juvenile, but offers some light relief from the boredom of a Sunday afternoon in prison.

Monday 1st Feb 2010.

Awake at 7.35am, off to the classroom above the gym for an hour testing my literacy levels. I am asked by the course tutor, Neil, to become the classroom assistant as it is obvious I am learning nothing new. I gladly agree which means I will remain at the gym every morning, it also looks great on my prison report.

Tuesday 2nd Feb 2010.

Nothing to report.

Wednesday 3rd Feb 2010.

Wide awake at 6.30. Rather than go back to sleep I get myself ready for the day ahead, and watch the dawn break. Having watched sunrise in some of the most fantastic places on earth while working on holiday programmes for television, this is as unremarkable as the place itself, but at least now I can add HMP Stafford to the list.

Trained hard in the gym today concentrating on cardio-vascular work, really beginning to feel the benefits.

The afternoon is spent at my job in the stores with Taff, and Scouse who is in his usual juvenile playful, but annoying mood. I become the object of his messing around when he begins chasing me around, simulating gay sex each time he catches me. Fearing his strange, amorous behaviour is getting out of control I became less patient with his game.

Later back on the wing Scouse pays a visit to my room and lies on my freshly laundered bed, making himself very much at home which annoys me. I tell him I don't appreciate him lying on my bed. He asks to borrow my hair cutting clippers which I politely decline as I don't want to get into the habit of lending out my personal stuff. I get the impression that to give an inch Scouse would take a yard, and I don't want to get into that sort of situation with him or anyone else.

While speaking to Jess, I'm disappointed to learn she won't be visiting tomorrow, she hasn't received a Visiting Order.

Thursday 4th Feb 2010.

Wake at 7.20am. The news reports a new design of unbreakable glassware for pubs. It shows images of a typical weekend night out when alcohol fuels violent attacks. GMTV interview a landlady who has been glassed in the face leaving her blind in her left eye after a young man attacked her. It brings back memories of my own incident,

315

and highlights what could have happened to me.

Today is the one year anniversary of Jess and I leaving our restaurant business.

Morning gym, afternoon in the stores.

Evening is spent in my room, I'm happy in my own company, but I am constantly visited by inmates who are keen to spend time in my company.

Friday 5th Feb 2010.

Morning in the gym. It's half day every Friday so the afternoon is spent on the wing. The sun is shining and it is pleasantly warm, so Mr. Hancock unlocks the gate, and allows us to roam the gardens. I chat with a chap called John Tierney. I learn that John was a customer of mine at the restaurant and enjoyed taking his wife there on a number of occasions. It turns out we know many of the same people. It is a very pleasant afternoon.

Saturday 6th Feb 2010.

Wake at 8.20am, decline a cooked breakfast.

10.00am an announcement over the tannoy invites inmates to a V.D.T. (Voluntary Drugs Test). Despite its title there's nothing voluntary about it, if you fail to attend the test it is noted in your prison file, and a veil of suspicion is cast over you. I happily provide a sample, and produce an immediate negative test result for cannabis, cocaine or heroin.

11.00am, John Tierney stops by my room for a chat. We discuss our Cat' D review and HDC (Home Detention Curfew) options. John and I are due to be considered at around the same time. Category D Open Prison is available to prisoners who qualify, my review is March 12th, but just over a month later I could be eligible for release on HDC. So, do I go to open conditions or wait for HDC? Open prison would mean dormitory style accommodation, but after twenty-eight days I'd be eligible for home visits, up to four days and nights a week at home, a way of re-introducing prisoners to society. John and I decide to cross that bridge when we come to it if we're given the option.

Sunday 7th Feb 2010.

I want to spend today on my own with my own thoughts. There are books I want to read, and letters I want to write. My door has been unlocked, but to make it clear I want to be alone I close and lock my door from the inside, thus indicating to most normal people *alone is what I want to be*. However, an annoying stream of visits begins at around 10.30am. If only I could lay my hands on a *Do Not Disturb* sign to hang from my door handle.

Monday 8th Feb 2010.

8.45am I report to the Education Dept. to take an English Literacy exam. The classroom is set out in a typical school classroom exam style, single tables in a row on which are placed a blank piece of lined paper, and a black biro. We are told we have an hour to answer forty questions. We all complete the exam in less than an hour. We're told the papers will be sent away to be marked and, if we pass, a certificate will arrive within three weeks.

Tuesday 9th Feb 2010.

Jess has come to see me today. It is great to see her, but the visit is over all too soon and I have that usual down-in-the-dumps feeling. Spend the evening frustrated that I can't get on with my life with Jess. My self-pity is interrupted with the usual inmates paying a visit to my room before it comes to my favourite part of the day, bang-up. Yes, I actually consider this to be the best part of my day. On my own, locked behind a door where no one else can bother me. Lights out 11.00pm.

Wednesday 10th Feb 2010.

2.20pm my probation officer visits along with prison officer Miss Badman and two young female trainee social workers.

My probation officer goes through my file and reports everything is looking good. He's paid a visit to see Jess at our new home and he has recommended to the prison that I be released on HDC (Home Detention Curfew) on the due date of 20th April. Although my reports are all good I am told by Officer Badman that I should be prepared to answer questions and concerns from the prison governor. The governor will have to consider the following:

1. Has this prisoner behaved well during incarceration?
2. Is this prisoner likely to re-offend while on HDC, or again in the future?

If this is the case then I'm confident I shall not have a problem being released on the 20th April.

I also learn that despite my custodial sentence ending on 1st September 2010 I will remain on Prison License until 1st September 2011. This means I will be required to report to the probation service at least once a month, and any employment offer has to be sanctioned by the probation service before being taken up. I am not allowed to leave the country during this time either. My plans to get engaged to Jess during a romantic break in New York are in tatters, this news is upsetting.

After the meeting I phone Jess to let her know that all has gone well, but we will be unable to take a holiday abroad for over a year. She responds in here usual positive way by saying;

"Well, Scotland is a great place to explore", but I can detect a certain amount of disappointment in her voice.

Thursday 11th Feb 2010.

Morning in the gym, afternoon spent sorting clean boxer shorts and socks in the store room.

Friday 12th Feb 2010.

Today I am summoned into Scouse's cell for a word. Someone has reported him for being too loud and going over the top. He's been warned about his behaviour and wants to know who's reported him. He is firmly pointing the finger at me and I try to assure him that I have had nothing to do with it. However, I am pleased to hear someone has reported him, perhaps the wing will be a little quieter now that he's been warned.

Saturday 13th Feb 2010.

Door is unlocked at 8.30am. Shortly after, I'm paid a visit by Iqbal, and Balal who inform me that a few of my neighbours have been called into the office and warned about their behaviour on the wing. My name was brought into the equation, it turns out someone has witnessed the constant visits to my room and has made a complaint on my behalf. I am advised that if it becomes a problem then one complaint from me and those people will be removed from the wing. I decide I will not be making any such complaint, and feel I am able to deal with these people myself. Since their warning the wing and visits to my room have been distinctively quieter.

2.30pm I call Jess. She tells me that she's been offered a job training a manager at a friend's lap dancing club in Oxford. My initial thought is disappointment, but I'm not surprised. I'm not happy with my partner working in a lap dancing club for obvious reasons, especially while I'm in prison, but there's nothing that I can do about it other than express my concerns. I have no right to tell Jess what she can and cannot do. When I met her eight years ago she'd worked her way up from manager to the Public Relations manager for the Spearmint Rhino group of clubs. I took her away from that with the dream of owning a successful restaurant business. That went very wrong, and I feel responsible. It has left us both with huge debts, and on that basis alone I don't have a leg to stand on when objecting to the offer of her new job. I convince myself I have nothing to worry about as I have no reason to distrust her, what will be, will be.

3.15pm my diary writing is interrupted with a polite knock on my door. It is Damian clutching an A4 sheet of paper. Damian welcomed me to G Wing with a spare copy of a TV guide he'd picked up from his job sorting newspapers. It may sound daft, but a TV guide is high on the list of luxury items in prison, and he was kind enough to give it to me. He did want something in return, however. He wants me to sign his A4 sheet of paper for his seventeen year old nephew, Jack, which I am more than happy to do. Damian stays for a pleasant chat for about half an hour. During this time I never do find out what he is in prison for. He says he prefers not to tell me, which I respect. Whatever he is in for, I consider Damian to be one of the more decent people I've met so far in prison, he is polite and considerate, generous, and has a good sense of humour. He was sentenced to thirty months, and he has less than three months remaining.

4.30pm, after dinner it's early bang-up, so I spend much of the evening replying to letters from friends. The thought of Jess returning to the seedy world of a lap dancing club isn't far from the front of my mind and locked behind a prison door only leads to a feeling of intense paranoia. My thoughts lead me to the ultimate question; do I want to be the boyfriend of a girl who works in a lap dancing club? The answer is definitely no. I decide this is how I'll put it to Jess when I next see her. Whatever money worries we have, it should not mean she has to resort to having to work in that environment, whether as a manager a trainer. I will tell Jess my concerns on the telephone tomorrow, I'm aware that I run the risk of her agreeing not to do the job, but then doing it anyway, how will I know? And if I did ever find that out, the deceit would destroy us. Lights out 11.00pm.

Sunday 14th Feb 2010. Valentine's Day.

Awake at 8.00am, speak to Jess around 11.00am to wish her a happy Valentine's Day and thank her for a hand-made Valentine's card she sent. I didn't mention my paranoia about her new job offer, it doesn't seem appropriate on this day. I've decided I'm in a situation where I cannot win, so it's best to just swallow that bitter pill.

Monday 15th Feb 2010.

Pretty uneventful day, nothing worth writing about.

Tuesday 16th Feb 2010.

1.45pm a visit by Jess. The visit is strained. The burning issue is that my girlfriend is about to take a job in her friend's lap-dancing club in Oxford. I air my concerns, struggling to put them in the most diplomatic way I can find, asking her to put herself in my shoes. Jess tries to reassure me that everything is going to be okay, and that her reasons for wanting to do the job are: 1. the money, 2. she enjoys it, 3. she's good at it and 4. she doesn't want to be sat in the house each weekend pining for me. Towards the end of the visit our discussion descends into an argument, something neither of us wanted to happen during the only ninety minutes of the week we spend in each other's company. We say our goodbyes, and I'm left feeling helpless and annoyed at the thought of my girlfriend having chosen to work in a club where men specifically pay to get sexually aroused. A club which is full of real arse-holes and fake boobs. How am I supposed to feel. Thanks for that Jess.

Wednesday 17th Feb 2010.

I wake at 7.20am after a restless night's sleep with thoughts of Jess circumnavigating my mind. At the gym I work out with John Tierney concentrating on building up the muscles in my arms and chest.

After lunch, work at the stores is busy and mostly conducted in silence. Scouse has decided not to talk to me at all after being warned about his behaviour on the wing once again. He has convinced himself that I'm at the centre of the complaints made against him. I have nothing to do with it. I can live without him talking to me, and his constant visits to my cell.

4.45pm dinner, an old favourite, sausage, egg, chips and beans, can't beat it.

7.00pm speak to Jess briefly as she is in Oxford having started her new job at her friend's lap-dancing club.

7.45pm banged-up, spend the evening watching TV and thinking about Jess.

Thursday 18th Feb 2010.

Work out at the gym during the morning.

1.45pm while the rest of the jail is on lock down due to staff training I, along with Banksy and Taff, are unlocked to attend work at the stores. I sort, fold, stack, and sweep to make the large store room less chaotic. We work hard all afternoon, and for our efforts we are rewarded with an *overachieved*, the first I've received. This will look great in my prison file and add weight in my favour when the governor considers releasing me early on HDC.

4.00pm back to the wing which gives me the opportunity to speak to Jess on the phone. Our conversation is back to normal and although I don't like her new job I've resigned myself to the fact there's sweet FA I can do about it so there's no point in dwelling on it.

Friday 19th Feb 2010.

Morning I spend at the gym training with JT (John Tierney), afternoon spend cleaning my room and hanging around the wing. Speak to Jess who takes twenty minutes trying to convince me that she will be okay at work at the lap-dancing club tonight, and that I have nothing to worry about. I try to heed her advice. 4.45pm bang-up for the next sixteen hours.

Saturday 20th Feb 2010.

My door is unlocked at 8.30am, and despite having been behind it for the last fifteen and three quarter hours, I decide to stay here in the peace of my own company. However, it isn't long before I receive the first of a stream of visitors. Carl, a twenty-three year old lad from Telford, jailed for drug dealing and knife crime, stops by for a chat. Next is Balal and Iqbal who want some advice on leaking a story to the press about racial abuse in prison. Then Marjorie from the chapel checks in to see how I'm getting on. No sooner has she left, than JT and Mark Botfield turn up to talk about the gym.

12 noon means lunch is served and we are banged up until 2.00pm. I phone Jess, apprehensive about how her first night at the club has gone. She is pleased to report that all is well and that I have nothing to worry about, and she'll be there again tonight.

My evening is spent wondering what the love of my life is getting up to at this club in Oxford. Thoughts like these can send an incarcerated man crazy, and I'm using all the will power I can muster to prevent this from happening. Lights out 11.00pm.

Sunday 21st Feb 2010.

Wake at 8.30am with my door being unlocked. I've spent much of the night awake thinking about what Jess could be up to. I am not in the best of moods, but try to be patient with another constant stream of visitors to my room. I just want to be left alone.

3.00pm I call Jess and wake her from sleep. She sounds rough, like one does after a good night out. Despite my suspicions Jess does a good job of reassuring me and dealing with my insecurities by telling me how much she loves me, and that she is not interested in meeting anyone else, especially in that environment.

4.00pm, we're served an early dinner followed by bang-up at 4.30pm, peace, no visitors.

Monday 22nd Feb 2010.

Nothing to report this day.

Tuesday 23rd Feb 2010.

I am required to complete a form entitled Re-categorization, Review & Application. I tick the box asking to be considered for category D status, meaning that I could be sent to an Open Prison.

1.45pm I am taken to the visits block. Jess has brought along Steve Dyson, former editor of the *Birmingham Mail* newspaper. It isn't the usual visit. Jess and I want answers as to why the *Birmingham Mail* has taken the line they have when covering my story, and aren't more supportive of me. What have I done to upset them? I suggest he would have sold more copies had the paper been in support of my case, and begun a popular debate on the anti-social behaviour of young people. Jess vents her anger at the way the paper treated my story, and makes it clear to Steve Dyson that he is ultimately responsible. She makes it clear, in no uncertain terms, that she isn't happy. Steve has moved on from the paper and now works with my old colleagues at *BBC Radio WM* where he hosts a show called *Hard Talk*. He invites me on as a guest to tell my story when I'm released, I happily accept.

Wednesday 24th Feb 2010.

At the gym I'm invited onto a Fitness For life course starting next week. This is a full time course and will mean I would have to give up my job in the stores department. I am pleased to accept though as this means I will no longer be required to sort boxer shorts and socks, a job that doesn't fill me with great enthusiasm. Instead I'll be at the gym morning and afternoon becoming extremely fit.

Talking to Tristan, he reckons my celebrity status is working in my favour. He has never heard of anyone being invited onto the *Fitness For Life* course, and suggests favouritism is taking place here. I point out that since joining the gym I have worked hard. I have become a classroom assistant, and even helped clean the gym when they are short of hands from time to time, I suggest that this hasn't gone unnoticed by the gym officers, and perhaps I'm being rewarded for my hard work, not favouritism.

Thursday 25th Feb 2010.

After lunch I attend my last shift at the stores. Scouse decides he can remain tight-lipped no longer, and breaks his silence towards me. He is intrigued to know who my extra visitor was the other day (Steve Dyson), he assumes he is a reporter. I answer his questions by being aloof, after all, it is none of his business. This annoys him and he becomes verbally aggressive to the point where an officer has to intervene with a warning. I suggest to Scouse that, for whatever reason, I seem to rub him up the wrong way, and perhaps it will be better if he reverts to not speaking to me, even this upsets him. But I'm happy in the knowledge that I won't be working with Scouse again after today.

I call Jess at the usual time, 7.00pm. She's in Oxford working at the club and announces that she'll be staying in Oxford tonight at her friends flat as she'll be working in Oxford the next day for Red Bull. This sets alarm bells of paranoia ringing for me, and in the privacy of my mind I question whether there's more to it than she's telling me.

Friday 26th February 2010.

Spend the morning working out in the gym. The only job for the afternoon is to collect the dirty laundry from E and F wings and drag them to the laundry department. As we arrive there are only two trollies, one overflowing with dirty laundry, the other only half full. Despite being of bigger build than me, Scouse immediately grabs for the half full trolley leaving me to struggle alone with the other. As we make our way to the laundry department Banksy helps Scouse with his half full trolley choosing to ignore me struggling, and Taff refuses to help at all, instead preferring to just walk alongside smoking a cigarette. The officers just turn a blind eye to what is going on. When we reach the off-load point, despite there being plenty of hands again, I am left to deal with unloading the over-full trolley alone. It is obvious that the only black guy in the group is being left without help, and this is noticed by a female officer. When she asks Scouse to lend a hand he begins arguing with her, and by the time their argument is over I have off-loaded my trolley. When we get back to G Wing the female officer reports Scouse to Mr. Hancock.

The rest of the afternoon is spent chatting to JT and Mark until 4.30pm when we are banged up.

Saturday 27th Feb 2010.

Usual stream of visitors begins shortly after my door is unlocked at 8.30am. Among the topics of conversation I learn about "plugging". Plugging is a means by which to smuggle stuff, drugs and phones, into jail. I learn the technique of plugging a phone. Take the battery out and insert a piece of paper or card to prevent the battery from making a connection with the power prongs when replaced. Wrap the phone in tissue, then wrap this in cling film or a small plastic bag to make it waterproof. Smother the package in lubrication, baby oil or body moisturizer will do and insert into the rectum. Once inside, use a finger to push the package to the back of the rectal passage, there's a ledge at the bottom of the spine, this ensures the package doesn't slip out when you sit down. I learn the largest phone this particular inmate has plugged is a Nokia 3310.

Sunday 28th Feb 2010.

Sundays in prison are long and extremely boring days. There is nothing to do but watch telly and read. Others prefer to play pool, darts, cards and board games. Idle minds search desperately for things to do. I am perfectly okay in my own company, however, others need to be surrounded by people, and again my room is the destination for a constant flow of bored prisoners looking for someone to talk to.

I call Jess at 2.30pm, she sounds dreadful and blames it on a sore throat. I believe it's more evidence of a party lifestyle, and fear she is becoming used to her freedom and independence.

The evening passes slowly, I turn my lights out at 10.00pm, the end of another month behind bars.

Monday 1st March 2010.

Wake at 7.30am, the start of my sixth month in prison. Head off to begin the full time course at the gym. Play badminton and soft tennis for much of the morning.

The afternoon is spent much the same but this is so much better than working in the stores.

Tuesday 2nd Mar 2010.

I wake to the news of friend and colleague Kristian Digby's death. Kristian was the presenter of BBC's To *Buy Or Not To Buy* property programme, and often used my restaurant to film in. Though Kristian wasn't the closest of friends the news knocks me for six.

8.30am the *Fitness For Life* course begins with a bleep test where I have to run between two markers while a CD plays a series of beeps. The task is to hit each marker on the beeps which become more frequent. Sounds simple, but it's exhausting. This is followed by sit ups, press ups and so on. I score 8.4 during the beep test, the idea being that in three weeks at the end of the course I will have improved my fitness levels and the score.

After lunch I receive a visit from Jess who looks amazing. We hold hands and chat about our future. We try not to pin our hopes on my being released early on HDC, but it's difficult not to. The ninety minutes flies by and it is time for the woman I love with all my heart to leave once again.

Weds 3rd Mar 2010.

7.22am as I try to get out of bed I am met with the pain of my newly exercised muscles. The fitness course has begun to do what it is designed to do.

8.30am I head to the education block where I am required to take a literacy exam. I have one hour to complete the paper of forty questions.

The afternoon sees a return to the fitness course to take part in a circuit. A circuit is a combination of short sprints, sit ups, press ups, star jumps and weights over a period of fifty minutes.

Thurs 4th Mar 2010.

Once again wake to the pain of muscles I didn't even know I have, I ache from head to toe and feel like crap. Luckily, in the gym we are given a free session to do what we like. I choose to play a few games of badminton, though it does take a while before my bruised muscles begin to un-seize.

Friday 5th Mar 2010.

The start of another long, boring weekend ahead, nothing to report this day.

Saturday 6th Mar 2010.

Wake at 8.30am, I feel dreadful. Along with aching muscles, the on-set of *man flu*. Chesty cough, headache, shivers, runny nose, the lot. I am determined to stay in bed, and lock my door from the inside telling all visitors to go away. I only venture from my room to collect meals and to phone Jess.

During our conversation Jess tells me she's agreed to work at the lap-dancing club again tonight. What first started as a couple of shifts training a manager to do the job as a favour to a friend has now turned into something more substantial. I fear she's enjoying her old job, and it's only a matter of time before she meets someone new.

4.30pm and we're banged up for the evening. By now my throat feels like I've attempted to escape by chewing through the razor wire. Were I at home I'd be sipping on hot lemon and honey immersed in a hot soothing bath. No such luxury here though. Lights out 11.00pm.

Sunday 7th Mar 2010.

8.30am, still feeling like crap I decide I'm going to take a more active role in the day, rather than lying suffering in my bed. I start with a hot shower, and shave a two day growth from my face. Next to get cleaned is my room. I vacuum, dust and polish the floor using a buffer. My door is wide open giving way to other inmates who cannot resist competing with each other to give me advice on how to achieve the best shine on my floor.

10.30am the wing gates are opened allowing us to enjoy the gardens on a gloriously sunny, but cold day. We stroll around chatting, very pleasant.

2.30pm I call Jess to get the latest steer on her night at the lap-dancing club. She assures me that all is fine, I have nothing to worry about, and that she can't wait to have me home again. I feel pathetic to require this constant reassurance, but it's a side-effect of being in this place.

Mon 8th Mar 2010.

7.30am I feel so much better than I have done recently. I'm feeling upbeat and positive. At the gym there is another circuit to complete. The afternoon is spent playing Volleyball against the gym officers, good team bonding.

Tuesday 9th March 2010.

Jess makes her usual weekly appointment to visit me. The visit is upbeat, we laugh and looked forward to when this nightmare will be over, we make plans, and discuss wedding thoughts.

Weds 10th Mar 2010.

Awake at 6.43am. A breakfast of *Weetabix*, honey, and raisins, sets me up for another fitness circuit at the gym. While there another random drugs test is carried out on each gym member, I pass, a few others fail.

After lunch play badminton and work out with JT. I've really settled into the gym routine and am enjoying it. The gym is run noticeably different from the rest of the prison, the attitude of the officers is much more respectful and this is reciprocated by the inmates. It means the days are much more bearable, and when I consider what I've been through so far in prison I feel privileged to be at the gym, most definitely the best place to be while in jail.

I'm feeling apprehensive, I'm awaiting a decision about whether I'm going to be moved to a Category D open prison, or released on Home Detention Curfew, the waiting and not knowing is becoming difficult to deal with.

6.30pm I phone Jess, she's on her way to Oxford to work at the club. I can't put my finger on it but there is something odd about the conversation, I put it down to being paranoid and remind myself to trust Jess and this new job. But it's worth making a note of this feeling in this diary as, if it does turn out to be what my gut is telling me, then at least I'll know to trust my gut feeling more in the future.

Back in my room Carl Wilson pays a visit for a chat. He gives me an insight into his life growing up in Telford, Shropshire. He says he always carried a cleaver knife for protection, and was forced to stab someone in the thigh once. He continues with stories of when he and his mates would roam the streets with nothing to do, then the group would place bets on how many drunken blokes they could find and knock out. How his friend went too far during one bet and had killed a bloke with a single punch. Carl is not much older than the youths who'd caused trouble at my restaurant. Carl's stories give me a scary insight into what was going through the minds of the youths who'd attacked me.

Thurs 11th Mar 2010.

The headlines in the news today remind me of the interesting chat I had last night with

Carl. Each news programme leads with the story of David Askew who was killed by a group of youths, an eighteen year old man has been arrested. The headlines read; *He lost his life because he would not, and could not fight back.* This brings to the forefront of my mind my own case, and as long as the law sides with the youths in an attempt to keep them out of the criminal system then, sadly, I fear there'll be more stories like this to come.

Friday 12th Mar 2010.

Morning is spent on the fitness course at the gym. Afternoon is spent wasting time as best I can.

Saturday 13th Mar 2010.

Another uneventful day.

Sunday 14th Mar 2010. Mother's Day.

I lost my Mum to cancer when she was just fifty-eight, ten years ago, and there's not a day that goes by that I don't think about that incredible woman. Mother's Day, therefore, isn't the best day of the year for me, so I choose to keep myself to myself as much as I can today.

Monday 15th Mar 2010.

Nothing to report

Tuesday 16th Mar 2010.

My mood today has unexpectedly taken a huge dip. I feel unenthusiastic, demotivated, and all round pissed off. No matter how hard I try I cannot lift my spirits from this depression.

Jess pays her weekly visit, however, I don't get to see her until 3.00pm leaving only an hour in each other's company. She does a great job of lifting my mood, but it's time for her to go and for me to return to my depression. It's horrible.

7.15pm I call Jess to be sure she got home safely, and to apologize for being in the dumps. She totally understands and tries to keep me positive. Jess is a great support.

I watch TV until I turn my light out at about 10.00pm. As I drift off to sleep an uncontrolled tear leaves my eye and rolls down my cheek before being absorbed into the pillow.

Wed 17th Mar 2010. St Patrick's Day.

I'm woken at 7.40am with Dave from the education department tapping on my door to inform me that I have a math's exam to sit this morning rather than go to the gym.

9.00a.m., in exam conditions, I answer forty questions within the allotted time of one and a quarter hours. I return to the wing where a pile of my freshly laundered clothes and bed linen await. Another luxury of being on G Wing. Wednesday is laundry day, all I have to do is fill my laundry bag with my dirty garments and drop it off at the small laundry room on the wing. It's returned to my room clean, and folded, bliss.

After lunch, it's back to the gym. Play volleyball, win five games, lose three. It is great fun and helps lift my depressed mood.

Thursday 18th March 2010.

I am given a date for my HDC board; the 16th April. This instantly lifts the dark cloud which has been over me for the duration of my stay here, at last there's a chink of light at the end of this extremely dark tunnel. It's still a long way in the distance, but at least I have something to aim for.

During association I call Jess to impart this piece of good news which lifts her spirits too. She wants me home now, and tells me how lonely she feels. I respond by saying;

"As long as your loneliness doesn't send you into the arms of another man."

She assures me that she has no intention of seeing anyone else, her words deal with my insecurities once again.

Friday 19th March 2010.

Another long and boring weekend ahead. The pleasant, warm spring sunshine is the highlight.

Wednesday 24th March 2010.

The gym officers ask me to design a circuit for the group in the gym. It consists of twenty stations, each with a different exercise to complete before moving onto the next. I am then asked to take the class, twenty-eight inmates to control and motivate through the circuit. Armed with a whistle and Officer Cooper's wristwatch I am in my comfort zone with an audience in front of me. I run around shouting timings and words of encouragement to complete each exercise. During the circuit the Number One Governor, Mr. Small, enters the sports hall to witness us all working hard and me in control. Being aware that this is the man who, in a couple of weeks, will take the decision whether to release me early or not I am keen to impress him, and this is my chance. I acknowledge him by saying good morning as I jog past on the circuit. He responds with a smile, job done.

After the circuit is complete, in the de-brief, Officer Cooper and my class of twenty-eight praise my efforts on a good circuit, and nickname me Mr. Motivator. During the shower that follows I am doused with a large bucket of cold water, this is a compliment in prison, a sign of acceptance, and I feel very much part of a team.

Thought of the day: *Only a life lived for others is a life worth living.*

So, my time inside continues in a similar routine day by day with me trying as much as possible to keep myself to myself and making a contribution to the prison system where I can, so it all looks good in my prison file, and with the hope of getting out of this hell-hole at the earliest opportunity.

Wednesday 31st March 2010.

The atmosphere of G Wing has been relaxed and quiet since Scouse was warned about his behaviour a few weeks ago. However, while relaxing in my room during this evening Scouse knocks on my door and I stupidly let him in. He is clearly very bored and takes the opportunity to revert to his formers ways, behaving more like a delinquent seven year old rather than a fully grown twenty-three old man. My patience runs out when, while sitting on the table where I write this diary and eat my food, he chooses to break wind. My small room is filled with the most disgusting smell ever produced by a human being, so much so that I can feel the contents of my stomach start to make its way north. He leaves my room, laughing, and proud of his pathetic performance.

Thursday 1st April 2010.

During lunch Scouse enters the doorway to my room, uninvited as usual. Given his behaviour yesterday I ask him to leave and to never visit my room again. As he tries to make his way further into my room I block him, he barges his way through me. I become angry, but he refuses to leave. Scouse stands at six feet two inches tall, is of large build, and weighs around eighteen stone. I am no match for the brute, but I choose to stand my ground. He too becomes angry, is this the excuse he's been looking for? He puts his forehead against mine, we are nose to nose, he is grunting like an angry boar, his breath is as disgusting as when he broke wind yesterday. He threatens to bite my nose off, and I push him away saying he doesn't scare me. Little does he know that deep inside I am preparing my nervous system for the pain of being hit anytime soon. My doorway becomes the view point for Banksy and other inmates who've heard our raised voices. Scouse tells Banksy to shut the door. Scouse removes his glasses and continues his threats, despite his size I am not going to back down, to do so will mean my life won't be worth living for the remainder of my stay. I prepare myself for one almighty battle, he'll almost certainly win, but I'm not going down without a fight. I'm also not going to be the one who throws the first punch, that will give him the ammunition he needs to have me nicked, I'm gonna do nothing to jeopardize my chance of HDC. I glance at the closed door considering my escape from this situation, the rectangular window is crammed with faces, potential witnesses. Realizing he's getting nowhere and I'm not about to back down Scouse chooses to leave my room protesting loudly to others that I'd called him a white bastard. Of course, I'd done no such thing. When Officer Preece arrives to establish what is going on I tell him only half the story. Despite what has happened, I don't want to be the one responsible for getting Scouse kicked off the wing, given time he'll do that himself. Instead I ask that he be told never to enter my room and I'll be happy with that.

Friday 2nd April 2010. Good Friday

There's nothing good about it. Today marks seven months behind bars which feels more like seven years. There's no work today and the time drags by. I'm taken to reception to pick up a parcel of motorcycle magazines my good friend and fellow biker James Parsons has thoughtfully sent in. These help to pass the time but evoke memories of our annual European biking trips which I'll miss out on this year. Man and machine, ultimate freedom, a stark contrast to my present predicament.

Saturday 3rd April 2010.

Am woken at 7.00am by the night guard switching my light on to check that I haven't dug my way out of the cell overnight. Spend the day wasting time the best way I can. The day seems to pass by with pace, 4.45pm time to be banged up for the evening. I settle to watch a film at 8.00pm. I make a cup of tea which I plan to drink with a bar of chocolate I've put on the window sill with the window open, this way it will be chilled by the crisp spring air, a treat I've been looking forward to. However, as I reach for the chocolate I

351

accidentally push it out of the window and it falls to the ground. Talk about taking candy from a baby, the disappointment is overwhelming. It's not unlike the scene in *Charlie And The Chocolate Factory* when Charlie is given his grandfather's last coin to buy a Srumdiddlyumpshush bar in the hope of finding the last Golden Ticket. Remember, all emotion is exaggerated in prison and this is no exception. I am a finger away from pressing the emergency button in my room to ask the night officer to retrieve it for me, but fear it won't look good in the handover notes in the morning. So I go without and consign myself to the fact that my chocolate bar has gone forever, it'll probably be picked up by one of the officers and never be seen again.

Sunday 4th April 2010. Easter Sunday.

I wake with thoughts of my chocolate bar on my mind, and as soon as my door is unlocked I ask whether I can retrieve it. This is pathetic, I convince myself that it is only a chocolate bar that cost forty-four pence, let it go. As I begin to watch the *Formula One Grand Prix* the tannoy crackles into action; "*EXERCISE*", I can't resist any longer, on go my shoes and, at speed, I make my way to the gate. Mr. Hancock is amazed to see me appear so quickly, and I explain what has happened. There it is, directly under my second floor window, still fully wrapped, but broken and chilled to perfection after its night on the tiles. I return to my room satisfied that my chocolate bar and I are re-united. As I write this diary entry, I'm looking at it, and have to consider my bizarre behaviour!

Lunch is served at 11.45am, Ham and pasta salad, we're each given a Cadbury's Creme Egg by Mr. Hancock who wishes us a happy Easter. What a generous and pleasant surprise, is this really prison?

I spend the rest of the afternoon making my way through The Sunday Times including all the supplements. Occasionally glancing at my chocolate bar, firmly grounded and ready for consumption later.

I phone Jess at 3.30pm, she tells me that she plans to go out with the girls tonight. I can't help but feel envious, an ugly emotion, but I can't help it. Jess is, after all, allowed to have a life, and as long as she doesn't kiss any boys while she's out then I have nothing to worry about.

Lights out 12.30am.

Monday 5th April 2010. Bank Holiday

There's no work today as it's a Bank Holiday so I try to stay in bed for as long as possible, but 9.30am sees the first of my visitors knocking at my door for a chat.

Despite knowing Jess has been on a *girlie-night* out last night, I decide to give her an early call. Now, I have to be honest, I do this for no other reason than to check that she made it home last night, and is home alone. I call her mobile, no answer, I call again, still no answer. I call a third time and it goes straight to voicemail. I become suspicious, why isn't she answering her phone? Why has she switched it off? Who is she with? Prison does this to a man. I call again fifteen minutes later, this time Jess answers sounding dreadful. I can understand only every third word she is saying, she is clearly still very drunk. I strain my ears to pick up any signs of background noise, a male voice perhaps, but I can only hear Jess's best friend Helen, I'm relieved, Jess is at our new house with her best friend, hung-over but safe, my paranoia can now cease, surely?

Jess reports that her night out was spoiled by the amount of people who enquired as to how I was getting on. This meant Jess was constantly reminded that I am in prison and couldn't just forget about it for a few hours and let her hair down. Of course, she's entitled to a night out, to relax and enjoy herself with her friends, but it is also very difficult for us both. Jess is a very attractive woman and no doubt is getting lots of attention when she's out, I trust her totally but being in here I've developed this paranoia which is killing me from the inside. I am unable to make rational thoughts, and I feel I cannot deal with this for much longer. I consider ending our relationship as I'm convinced it's the fairest thing to do, to allow Jess to get on with her life without the burden of me. Lights out 11.00pm.

Tuesday 6th April 2010.

1.45pm am taken to visits block for a visit from Jess. She looks amazing and I'm so happy to see her. She tells me all about her night out, and as usual it seems this paranoid depressive has been over thinking things. I tell her how anxious I am if the decision is taken not to release me early,

355

but Jess reassures me, in her usual clever way, that she'll still wait another five months for my return if she has to.

Lights out 11.00pm.

Friday 9th April 2010.

Off to the gym for the final of the *Fitness For Life* Course test. My objective is to beat all previous beep test scores over the last five weeks, and I'm pleased to say that I not only beat them, but more than double my score. This is the fittest I've been since childhood, result.

The afternoon is spent on the wing, and in the gardens enjoying the first of the warm spring sunshine. My peace is disturbed by Banksy who's become the latest victim of the Facebook phenomenon. His fiancé has announced she's met a Portuguese chap on the networking site. Needless to say, he's distraught, and although he is a trained prison Listener he himself is in need of someone to talk to, and I'm happy to lend an ear and a shoulder on which to cry.

Saturday 10th April 2010.

Another gloriously sunny and warm day which means nothing other than to remind me of what I'd be doing if I were not surrounded by these twenty feet high, razor-wired walls.

After lunch I'm handed a letter, it's from my probation officer who has made an appointment to visit me to discuss any anxieties I may have prior to my release. Could this mean I'm definitely going home early? I read the letter again and again searching for the smallest clue which might confirm this.

Sunday 11th April Jess's birthday.

My door is unlocked after fifteen hours at 8.30am, I immediately call Jess to sing happy birthday down the phone, but I'm disappointed, there's no answer. The morning is spent roaming the gardens. As beautifully maintained as they are they do nothing to help my feelings of deep depression. It's Jess's birthday, I should be with her.

1.45pm Jess visits, yes, on her birthday she wanted to visit me in prison, what a girl. It is great to see her and hear about her adventures over the last week. She plans to go out for birthday drinks tonight, and I fall deeper into a depressive state again. I should be celebrating her birthday with her. No matter how hard I try I can offer no enthusiasm for Jess's birthday. Jess leaves at 4.00pm, no doubt wondering why she's bothered to spend time with me given the mood I am in.

Back in my room I spend another boring evening locked behind my door, pissed off and anxious to be home. Lights out 9.30pm

Wednesday 14th April 2010.

9.00am I am taken to the visits block to meet my probation officer. The meeting lasts two hours, during which I am asked questions about how I've been getting on in prison, about my offence, and what I have planned for the future. My probation officer can't say for certain that I'll be granted early release on HDC, but she does confirm that my board will be taking place this Friday, the 16th April, and that all parties are in support of my application. Great news, surely I'll be home soon.

After lunch I attend the gym to work out with JT. I am paid a visit by Steve the prison probation officer who confirms that my HDC board will be taking place this Friday at 2pm. He takes me through various bits of paperwork and reports that I have a good clean prison record so it should all be very straight forward. I'll sit the board on Friday, confirmation will be by the following Tuesday, the people who fit the electronic monitoring device to my ankle upon release need forty-eight hours' notice, so I could be home by next Friday he tells me. This is the best news ever. I become very excited but have to err on the side of caution, I won't believe it until I'm the other side of these prison walls in Jess's arms.

I call Jess at the earliest opportunity with the good news and although she's excited, she too shares the same apprehension as I do and we try hard not to pin our hopes too high.

Thursday 15th April 2010.

Visit from Jess this afternoon, we're both excited but apprehensive about my board tomorrow. For the first time in a long time we can actually begin to see an end to this nightmare.

Back on the wing I prepare as best I can for tomorrow's board. I gather together all my certificates from the various courses I've completed and exams I've passed. I make a detailed diary of what I will be doing with my days should I be released early, I have my hair cut, and I'm set to make a good impression to the board.

Friday 16th April 2010.

I spend the morning in the gym, I am in a great mood and apprehensively looking forward to this afternoon's board.

It isn't until 2.30pm that I am collected by an officer and, armed with my file of good behaviour evidence, I am escorted to a part of the prison I've never been to before. Apart from the steel bar gated entrance, it is a typical office setting. I am asked to wait in a reception area, I sit on comfy low chairs

and pick up a glossy magazine from a table in front of me. No sooner have I sat down and I am called through. I enter a room which looks like an old boardroom, long, shiny, mahogany table with fourteen high back leather chairs, seven each side. I am invited to sit at the head of the table. Facing each other sits Steve, the prison probation officer, and Governor Moreland. In front of him is my prison file upon which I notice some handwritten notes. Governor Moreland begins by saying;
"Right, the bad points against you are" and he lists three things.

"The good points are" he lists five things.

"It is for this reason we will be recommending you be released early on HDC, don't let me down Blake".

And that was it. The whole board took no longer than three minutes. I am told the procedure is that the Number One Governor, Mr. Small, has to sign it off on Monday, meaning that this time next week I could be at home. I float back to the wing to call Jess with the great news.

Monday 19th April 2010.

The following weekend is the usual boring one, but my head is full of excitement and plans for my imminent release. At the gym I find it hard to concentrate on anything. I keep watching the door for an officer to enter to tell me that I'll be going home this week. At one point Steve, the prison probation officer, does appear and my heart almost leaves my chest, but he is looking for someone else.

7.45pm time to be banged up for the night with Officer Major turning the key. Shortly after I've been locked away my door is unlocked again. It is Mr. Hancock who is just about to finish his shift and won't be in for another week. He's been given word that I've been recommended for early release, and he wants to say goodbye and wish me well. I thank him for all his support and hope to see him again, but obviously in much better surroundings. Mr. Hancock is by far the best officer I've met in prison, it says a lot about his character when he goes out of his way to say goodbye, cheers Mr. Hancock, and I hope Man' City pull it out of the bag for you.

Tuesday 20th April 2010.

The day I've been longing for since the start of my sentence. Today is HDC day, my earliest opportunity of release from this hell, the day I believe I'll be going home to begin the rest of life. I head off to the gym hoping for my session to be interrupted by an officer with the news that I'll be going home sometime very soon, but no such luck. During lunch time Mr. Major asks whether I've had word yet and is surprised that I haven't. He agrees to chase a decision for me. By the evening he too has heard nothing. Another evening of tension and frustration.

Wednesday 21st April 2010.

I have slept barely a wink all night. My door is unlocked by Mr. Major at 8.20am, he is clutching a piece of paper. It is an email from the Governor requesting proof of my employment upon release before making his final decision. When I had completed my application for release on HDC a few months ago, a section on the form asked for details of what I'll be doing with my time should I be released early, I completed the form with details of working on a programme I have written called *Behind The 9's*, I will produce this through my own company Ashley Blake Ltd. The Governor wants proof that Ashley Blake Ltd really does exist. He wants the Company Registration Number, VAT Registration Number, and company letterhead. I phone Jess at 8.30am, she'll be able to fax that information through in an instant. Jess usually works from our office at home most of the time, however, this morning when I phone she's already half-way to a meeting in Northampton, great. Jess agrees to call my accountant who can fax the required information through to the prison.

HM Prison Service

MEMORANDUM:

HDC

From   HDC Clerk

Tel No.

To   Blake – A3043AH

Date   19 April 2010

Location G2-010

Further to your recent HDC board a decision with regard to your release on HDC is partly dependant upon your planned employment upon release.
The Governor requests that you provide further evidence of your production company Ashley Blake Ltd, for example letter heads, VAT registration etc.
When I have received this information the Governor will make a final decision.

Sue Huxley

At lunch time I call Jess again to ask whether she's been able to talk to my accountant and get the ball rolling, but there's no answer. Two, three, four attempts, still no answer. I can see a prison officer making his way down the corridor to lock us up over lunch time, I frantically dial the number again, this time Jess answers, but says she's only got ten seconds, this is not enough time so I'm left with no option but to agree to call her again later. I head off to my room accepting that I'll be here for another week at least. Mr. Major is very helpful providing me with a fax number, but with Jess on the road the information the Governor needs to make his decision will not be faxed until tomorrow. It's so frustrating but there's nothing I can do, my fate is in the hands of other people.

Thursday 22nd April 2010.

I head off to the gym and spend the time watching the door for an officer to appear with good news for me, but still nothing. During association I have the first opportunity to phone Jess. She tells me that last night she made a hundred and twenty mile round trip to home to fax the information to the prison, and that she phoned the prison today to confirm that the documents have been received. What a girl, I owe her big time.

Friday 23rd April 2010.

Spend the day on tenterhooks hoping for an answer, but by 3.30 I've consigned myself to the fact that I won't by going home any time soon, and that I ought to stop anticipating it, this will only lead to huge disappointment.

4.30pm, dinner and early bang-up. I watch the evening news to learn that my old pad-mate at Winson Green, Sunil, together with Spencer, and his Dad Raj have been found guilty of smuggling drugs with a street value of six million pounds, they have been sentenced to upwards of five and a half years.

Thought of the day; *Hate the sin, but not the sinner.*

Sat 24th April 2010.

Nothing to report.

Sunday 25th April 2010.

Jess visits this afternoon. She is full of plans for our new home, and very much looks forward to having me there soon, but with no news of my release it is increasingly hard to look forward to our future. At 4.00pm it is time for her to leave me again. We both say our goodbyes, each hoping the next time she leaves Stafford Prison I'll be leaving with her. Soon after I arrive back on G Wing dinner is served, and I'm locked behind my door. I lie waiting for time to pass, paranoia sets in forcing me to believe, for whatever reason, Governor Small isn't going to release me any time soon. I am beginning to struggle to stay positive, and battling to stay sane, I feel like bursting with frustration.

Monday 26th April 2010.

Today I learn that I'm to have a second board to sit this coming Friday. This means I am not going home this week, at least I can now just get on with it as opposed to anxiously waiting for an answer.

Tuesday 27th April 2010.

During my session at the gym I'm told stories of other inmates being released soon after attending their second board which helps to keep me positive.

Friday 30th April 2010. Bank Holiday weekend

I'm told that I won't be attending a second board after all. Instead, my papers with the new information will be put before the number one Governor Mr. Small for his consideration.

At the gym I am surrounded by a small group of guys who are chatting about cars, and how much money they have. One member of the group knows that I drove a Range Rover, and the conversation turns to how much money they think I have, and whether it would be worth kidnapping me for ransom. I'd like to think that they are joking, but I also feel that many a true word is spoken in jest.

The spot light turns to another member of the group who begins boasting about the lengths he's gone to in previous criminal encounters. He confesses that he doesn't think twice about doing what it takes to get what he wants, and recounts an occasion when, whilst burgling a house in an affluent area of Birmingham, he came across a young mother. He asked her for the combination to the safe, and when she repeatedly refused he took a small baby from a cot in the nursery, placed it in a pillowcase, and threatened to bounce the baby off every wall until the mother gave up the combination. He recounts his story with glee. The conversation continues, each trying to out-do the last with stories of their criminal career.

Sat 1st May 2010. Pinch Punch first of the month.

I wake at 8.30am after a good night's sleep. The wing is buzzing with news of Mossy. Having spent six years in prison Mossy was released two days ago on a temporary licence, but he is already back behinds bars after being caught fighting in a pub on his first night of freedom. I also learn that an inmate on E Wing has died overnight from a heart attack, he was due to be released the very next day.

Sunday 2nd May 2010.

The gates to the wing are unlocked, and exercise is announced at 10.00am. On the way out to enjoy some fresh air I notice a tall, attractive, mixed race woman talking to Officers. Once outside I learn that this woman is the new Governor of The Offender Management Unit, the department responsible for managing inmates' stay. I take the opportunity to introduce myself, and to ask whether a decision has been made with regard to my release. Although I've never met the woman she seems to know me, and informs me that a decision has been made, but the result lies with the HDC clerk, and because it's a Bank Holiday weekend I won't know the answer until at least Tuesday when the clerk returns to the office.

Monday 3rd May 2010.

Nothing to report this day.

Tuesday 4th May 2010.

After a difficult night's sleep I wake late at 8.49.am. I rush to get ready for the day ahead. Luckily I'm not the only one running late this morning; our doors haven't been unlocked yet. Today's the day for the big decision or at least I think it is. Within ten minutes of waking I am downstairs ready to go. I ask Mr. Rowlinson to ring across to the HDC clerk for an answer which he agrees to do, and will let me know at lunch time. Off to the gym at 9.15am, mind firmly on going home at the end of the week.

As I return to the wing at lunch time Mr. Rowlinson beckons me into the office. My heart begins to beat excitedly, but he tells me that the Governor wants more information. What more could he possibly want? I have given all the proof I have, and it's all genuine. Mr. Rowlinson is as confused as I am, but knows no more than he's told me, he suggests that I call my outside probation officer for the answers. Instead of taking lunch I decide to call Jess and ask her to call my probation officer. I agree to call Jess again at 1.45 pm, after lunch and I have been unlocked.

I spend lunch time confused and frustrated that this decision is not as straight forward as I thought it would be. My prison record is excellent, I'm low risk, I have a job to go out to, a secure loving home, surely I am an ideal candidate to be released early on HDC?

1.45pm I call Jess again who has spoken to my probation officer and she has the answers. The Governor is concerned about my plan for employment upon release. Before being sent to prison I spent my time writing programme ideas. I wrote *Behind The 9's*, about three of my good friends who are motorcycle paramedics with the West Midlands Ambulance Service. It goes like this:

Speed saves lives and if you're critically injured then you want the fastest medical help in town - The Motorcycle Paramedics. They can reach you quicker than anyone else and give you the medical help that could make the difference between life and death. This observational documentary series will concentrate on the three motorcycle paramedics of the West Midlands Ambulance Service and intimately follow their life saving work.

The plan is to complete research work on the idea and arrange to start filming the series. My role will be as producer/director using my own production company Ashley

Blake Ltd. I already have interest from Channel Five for a series of six programmes. However, the Governor has concerns about the legitimacy of my project and despite all the information I've given, apparently he still feels uneasy. I am told my application for release on HDC will be looked at again this coming Friday.

This afternoon's session at the gym is interrupted by Mr. Kavana, the prison probation officer who has a short list of specifications from Governor Small. I assure him of the answers and offer to go into more detail in a letter which he thinks would be a good idea. I agree to write the letter this evening, and he agrees to pick it up from the office in the morning and place it before Governor Small tomorrow.

I spend the evening writing a very detailed letter to Governor Small describing exactly what I will be doing in the production of *Behind The 9's*.

Wed 5th May 2010.

As agreed Mr. Kavana collects my letter for Governor Small.

Thursday 6th May 2010.

While the UK goes to the polls in a general election, life in prison takes the now all too familiar routine. This afternoon Jess pays a visit, the first in ten days. She looks great, and we enjoy our visit hoping that this will be her last one.

Friday 7th May 2010.

As I head into another weekend there's still no answer from Governor Small.

Saturday 8th May 2010.

Wake to a cold and miserable Saturday morning. The heating system has been turned off early meaning the room is cold so I spend much of the day under my duvet. Banged-up at 4.30pm for the night. I watch a film on the DVD channel called *The Last House On The Left*. I was surprised at the choice, it was a violent thriller with a long scene of the brutal rape of a seventeen year old girl. Totally inappropriate I think. Lights out 10.15pm.

Sunday 9th May 2010.

Nothing to report.

Monday 10th May 2010.

The start of another week, the start of more anxious waiting for a decision. I head off to the gym. Everyone is surprised that I'm still here, even the gym officers, I have no answers for them. During lunch time I'm told by Officer Emery that Governor Small and Governor Moreland are discussing my case today so an answer is imminent. By the evening still no answer.

Tuesday 11th May 2010.

I wake at 7.44am. Before heading off to the gym I ask Mr. Hancock to put in, what has by now become, the daily call to the HDC department for an answer. Due to new inductions the gym is full today, so I am sent back to the wing. I use my time to write letters. Spend much of the afternoon in Mark Walkers room chatting about the prison system. Mark is a former military man and G Wing's Number One, our conversation is interesting, and makes a refreshing change from the normal level of conversation.

4.30pm dinner is dished up, during which Mr. Hancock tells me that he's spoken to the HDC department who, in turn, told him that a decision is being discussed this afternoon. A familiar story I think, but Mr. Hancock agrees to chase them up again in the morning.

I spend the evening watching live coverage of Gordon Brown resigning, and David Cameron becoming the new British Prime Minister.

Thought of the day: *Often the good suffer and the wicked prosper.*

Wednesday 12th May 2010.

Wake at 7.30am after a restless night's sleep thinking about my situation. 8.45am I head off to the gym with Mr. Hancock agreeing to chase a decision on my behalf. Lunch time comes and goes with no answer. I ask Mr. Hancock whether I ought to begin the official complaint procedure. He advises me to leave it until next week. I call Jess only to hear the disappointment and frustration in her voice. She's visiting tomorrow.

Thursday 13th May 2010.

1.30pm I'm taken to the visits block, Jess is number thirty-nine on the list which means I don't get to see her until 2.50pm. She is so frustrated that I haven't been given a decision, and that the whole procedure is taking so long, she has complained to my solicitor. My solicitor agrees to write a letter of complaint to the Governor. This prompts me to do what I can, and after returning to the wing I complete a formal complaint form addressing it to the Area Manager of the prison service, briefly outlining my complaint.

Friday 14th May 2010.

The highlight of today is the delivery of the canteen, and as you can tell from my receipt, I've once again overdosed on comfort food, mainly chocolate.

Despatch Receipt 13/05/2010

Route/load: SF / 000616
Order Number: E5500000000000241355
Customer ID: A3043AH   1 of 2
Customer Name:

BLAKE A

Prison Name: HMP STAFFORD

Location: G-2-010

Product Description	Ord	Desp	Price
UB1 Phone Credit	5	5	5.00
Amber Leaf 25g	1	1	5.80
Swan Slm Filter Tip	1	1	0.75
Dove Stk Invis 40ml	1	1	2.49
Dove Bdy Wash 250ml	1	1	2.99
Wine Gums £1 170g	2	2	2.00
ES M/Choc 100g 44p	4	4	1.76
Bounty Milk Std	5	5	2.35
Mars Bar Std	2	2	0.88
Snickers Std	2	2	0.88
Cof Bombay Mix 100g	1	1	0.49
Tetley T/Bags 40s	1	1	1.39
HS Milk Semi 500ml	2	2	0.98
Dairylea PM109 140g	1	1	1.09
Banana	2	2	0.60
HS Frt S/cake 65p	1	1	0.65
R/E Shortbread 125g	1	1	0.75
JW Mack Filet/SF	1	1	1.19
JW Mack Fillet/Tom	1	1	1.19
DM Pear Hlv Jc 415g	2	2	1.98
HS P/app Sl Jc 227g	2	2	1.18

Total Ordered: 39
Total Despatched: 39   36.39

DO NOT OPEN BAGS UNTIL YOU HAVE CHECKED
THE CONTENTS. ERRORS CANNOT BE RECTIFIED
ONCE BAGS HAVE BEEN OPENED.

Saturday 15th May 2010.

Nothing to report.

Sunday 16th May 2010.

Awake at 8.30am, sit in the first of the warm sunshine I've seen in two weeks. Watch the Formula One Grand Prix, phone Jess, sit in the sun, 4.30pm dinner, and banged up. It is still bright with sunshine when I turn the TV off at 9.15pm, but I am keen to end yet another day wasting away behind these high walls and closer to my day of liberty.

Monday 17th May 2010.

I wake at 7.27am wondering what the week ahead will have in store for me, and whether this will be the week I go home.

At lunch time Mr. Hancock has spoken to the HDC department who tell him that a decision whether to release me is still being considered, they will let me know as soon as they are decided.

Tuesday 18th May 2010.

I wake at 7.30am under a dark cloud of depression. At the gym I haul myself through some sort of workout in the hope of releasing some of those feel-good endorphins, but no matter how hard I try I cannot muster enough enthusiasm.

During evening association the gates to the garden are unlocked allowing me to enjoy some evening sunshine, a rare and pleasant treat. When I phone Jess I learn she has been in much the same mood as me all day.

Wednesday 19th May 2010.

I have little enthusiasm for the gym today, I choose to read a book instead of working out. I'm joined by Gym Officer Hill (Little Hill as he's known). We get to talk about what has happened to me, and he shares some sympathy with the situation I was faced with on that fateful night. He also shares his own near-miss experience which could have ended the same way. We chat for well over an hour and cover many subjects. It makes a refreshing change to have a decent conversation with someone that doesn't involve the usual flow of bullshit which constantly dribbles from the mouths of the majority in here.

When I phone Jess during evening association she is excited. She's spoken to my solicitor who's sent a letter to the prison asking for a decision to be made within the next seven days. Jess has also spoken to my probation officer who has been contacted by the prison. My probation officer can't understand why there is a delay in my release, I have ticked all the correct boxes, and have all parties' support apart from the number one Governor, Mr. Small.

Thursday 20th May 2010.

I wake at 7.50am. Today marks a month since I was due to be released on tag, why are they keeping me here? It is ridiculous to spend taxpayers' money on keeping me locked away when there is absolutely no need. Punishment has been served in the cruelest way possible.

The day doesn't amount to much, and after checking in with Jess, I return to my room to be alone. Today is the hottest day of the year so far, my room is hot and stuffy, along with thoughts of my release swirling around my head I find it impossible to sleep.

Friday 21st May 2010.

At the gym I see the prison probation officer Mr. Kavana. He's just been given the latest on my release. He tells me that the Governor still has reservations about my planned employment believing my role to be too "high profile," and I am encouraged to seek alternative employment. This news angers me, the Governor has no right to dictate my employment. Journalism is what I do, making television programmes is what I do, if I were a builder there'd be no problem.

I decide to write another letter, and Mr. Kavana agrees to get it in front of Governor Small this afternoon.

Ashley Blake
A3043AH
G2-10

Friday 21st May 2010
Ref: HDC Board

Dear Mr. Small,

Further to my letter dated 3rd May 2010, it has been brought to my attention your concerns with my employment should you decide to grant my release on HDC.

As you are aware I intend to work on writing several programme ideas employed by my own company Ashley Blake Ltd. I have already supplied you with details of one particular idea, Behind The 9's television series. However, due to the delay in my release this programme is likely to be postponed as it will now be impossible to meet the deadline. I shall therefore now turn my attentions to other ideas at the writing and research stage. This will involve office based research using the internet and occasional visits to the library. Having spoken to my probation officer, I have been informed that there are several pieces of work I am required to complete which is also part of my plan whilst on HDC. I also intend to re-establish my plans to wed my long term partner, Jessica Hayes.

I am aware that there may be some media interest upon my release. During my initial board on the 16th April 2010, I assured Governor Moreland that despite this interest I would not be talking to any media outlet until my sentence is complete.

I understand your concerns and I want to assure you of my good intentions. I have thus far completed my sentence without any concern. I have participated in several courses and I have been employed in three trusted positions within this prison. My prison file should show that I have been a model inmate and someone who is keen to progress through the system. I am fully aware of my responsibilities whilst on HDC and I can assure you I intend to conduct myself in an active and proper manner.

With this further information, can I please urge you to make your final decision.

Yours faithfully

Ashley Blake

I want to explain in the letter that during my time here I have witnessed several inmates being granted HDC, some without any employment plans at all, others who have simply played the system by inventing offers of employment and getting friends or family members to verify it with a phone call. I think better of it.

1.45pm Mr. Kavana collects my letter as promised, and delivers it by hand to the Governor. Later this afternoon I am called into the wing office where Governor Moreland is waiting. He tells me that he is happy with my letter, and that he will be discussing it with Governor Small this afternoon, he is confident that I will have an answer early next week.

Saturday 22nd May 2010.

The weathermen are reporting the weekend as being the hottest of the year so far, and for once they are right. The day is spent sunning myself in the garden, and trying to keep as cool as possible.

4.30pm early bang-up, as always during weekends, fifteen and a half hours locked away behind a thick steel door in a small hot and very stuffy cell.

Sunday 23rd May 2010.

Jess comes to see me this afternoon, great to see her, very sad to see her leave. Back to a hot cell for another fifteen and a half hours locked away.

Monday 24th May 2010.

I wake at 7.48am, optimistic, wondering what this new week has in store for me. Will I be going home? Spend the morning at the gym working off the weekend chocolate gorge. Back on the wing at lunch time and there's good news for the forty residents. Scouse has been granted category D, and will be moving out of the prison this afternoon. It is difficult to work out who is more pleased, Scouse or his fellow G wingers. I am over the moon to see him go.

When I speak to Jess this evening it's obvious she's become extremely frustrated with the prison service. She's angry and upset that a decision has not yet been made. This living in limbo, the not knowing one way or the other, is cruel and unnecessary, but there's little either of us can do.

Tuesday 24th May 2010.

There's no gym today and I spend the morning trying to waste time. Having nothing to do soon allows thoughts of your situation to begin to eat at your subconscious. I have all but given up on hope of an early release. I flick through the

Christian calendar hanging from my cupboard door to work out how long I have left, worst case scenario, I count fifteen weeks to the day.

Wednesday 26th May 2010.

The day passes by in the usual routine of gym, lunch, then more gym, followed by dinner then association. When I phone Jess at the usual time of 7.00pm the conversation starts as it normally does;

"Hi, how's you? How was your day?"

Jess can't understand why I am sounding so normal. When I ask what she is talking about she tells me that she's spoken to my outside probation officer, and learned that my early release has been declined by Governor Small. This news hits me like a freight train, Jess is understandably upset, and I try, in vain, to cheer her up. It seems she had her hopes on having me home soon and so did I.

I return to my room floored by the news, but at least I now have a decision, and can begin the process of appealing it, I first need a reason as to why I have been refused an early release.

Lights out 11.00pm.

It is difficult to sleep tonight, the disappointment is fierce. Anger prevents me from dropping off. Lights back on, and I decide to fight back by writing a Press Release. My plan is to send it out addressed to my solicitor under Rule 39: *Any correspondence to your legal team is private and confidential,* meaning I can seal the envelope and prison staff cannot see its contents. I will instruct my solicitor to send my Press Release to all my media contacts in the hope of exposing this prison's cruel and unfair treatment towards me.

PRESS RELEASE:

Former BBC presenter Ashley Blake has lodged an appeal with the Prisons and Probation Ombudsman against a decision on early release.

The 40 year old, ex-newsreader was due for release on Home Detention Curfew on the 20th April this year, seven and a half months into a two year sentence for assault. However, a decision was taken not to release Blake on Tag by HMP Stafford's Governor Peter Small despite recommendations by the prison service and probation officers.

Although Blake was sentenced to two years behind bars at Birmingham Crown Court on 2nd September 2009 he will have to serve only half the sentence in jail. The time spent behind bars can be further reduced for good behaviour and whether he is considered no risk to the public. Mr. Blake was assessed and recommended for release on 16th April 2010 and was expecting to serve the remainder of his sentence under home detention curfew between 7.00pm and 7.00am. Despite recommendations for release by prison staff and probation officers Stafford's overall Governor took seven weeks to consider Blake's early release then declined without reason.

Speaking through his solicitor Mr. Blake said " I cannot understand why Mr. Small has taken such a hard line with me. Since arriving in the prison I have actively participated with everything that has been required of me. I have successfully completed several educational courses and been employed in three highly trusted positions. My prison record is exceptional. I have been a model prisoner. I have the support of a loving family, a stable *home and secure employment waiting for me. I am not a risk to society, therefore, I am keen to understand how I do not meet the criteria for early release".*

ENDS.

Thursday 27th May 2010.

My mornings are usually full of optimism, I am a morning person, especially during the lighter spring/summer months. I am usually raring to go. Today though, all optimism is depleted, I've been running on fumes for months, but now my tanks have run bone-dry. I am miserable and depressed. So much so I consider whether it is actually worth carrying on with this existence. Luckily, such thoughts are soon gone by the time I am on the treadmill at the gym.

At around 3.00pm I am working out with JT on the bench press when I am interrupted by a visit from Governor Moreland with the news that Jess has already given me. He gives me two pieces of A4 paper, and asks me to firstly read the one entitled *Reasons For Refusal of HDC*, it reads;

FORM HDC(6) NOTIFICATION OF REFUSAL OF HOME DETENTION CURFEW

Surname: **Blake**	Forename(s): **Ashley**
NOMS Number: **A3043AH**	Date of Birth: **15/07/1969**
Prison Number: **CN7762**	
Proposed address of curfew:	

You have been considered for release on Home Detention Curfew. It has however been decided, on the basis of the evidence available, that you should not be released on Home Detention Curfew. Reasons for this decision are given below.

Reasons for refusal of HDC:

In view of your proposed employment plans there are concerns that you may breach your curfew licence conditions.

Signed: _P. Morland_   Name: _MORLAND_

Grade: _PSM F_   Date: _27/5/10._

This is the answer I've been waiting six weeks for, Governor Small has finally made his decision.

391

The other piece of paper is a Form *Comp 1,
Prisoners Formal Complaint*. Governor
Moreland suggests I come up with another
plan for my employment, something that
doesn't include the high profile world of
television. I am asked to place the
completed form in the yellow box on the
wing before lock up tonight, and the night
staff will collect it for processing tomorrow.
Governor Moreland is very helpful, and
after dinner this evening I set about
completing the complaint form.

Friday 28th May 2010.

I wake up in much the same mood as
twenty-four hours previous. I've resigned
myself to the fact that I'll be residing in this
hell until September 1st, another fifteen
weeks away.

During this afternoon at around 3.30pm I
am called into the office. Governor
Moreland is waiting. He has a copy of my
Formal Complaint which he tells me he is
happy with what I have written, and is off
to see the number one Governor Mr. Small
shortly. I thank him for his help, but I hold
no optimism for a positive outcome. An
hour later we are locked behind our doors

to begin another long and very boring weekend in hell.

The wing soon falls silent as inmates settle in. The quietness is interrupted with the sound of footsteps along the landing. This is unusual because once we've been locked away there isn't usually any movement from the officers in the corridor, unless there's an emergency in one of the cells. This is no emergency, the footsteps amble along in no rush. My cell is the very last one along the corridor, and I hear the footsteps getting closer to my door. Then the key is in my door, the lock is turned, the door flung open. It is Mr. Major. He tells me Governor Moreland is in the office and wants to see me. I excitedly don my shoes, and make a swift and eager journey to the office. As I enter, Governor Moreland is leant against the desk with an expressionless face, he says with a disappointed tone in his voice;

"Well, I've been to see Governor Small, and he's made his decision".

I let out a disappointed sigh, Governor Moreland continues;

"And I can tell you that you're going home".

I want to throw my arms around Governor Moreland and jump up and down with joy, it is like nothing I have ever experienced. To be told you have your liberty back has got to be the biggest high. Instead, I shake the Governor's hand firmly, and thank him for his help with my complaint and, no doubt, for persuading his boss to see sense and let me go.

Now, this is another Bank Holiday weekend meaning the staff won't be back in the office until Tuesday when they will begin the process of my release. I could be home by this time next week. I phone Jess immediately, but no answer, she'll have to wait until tomorrow to hear my good news.

I head back to my cell where Mr. Major is waiting to lock me back up;

"What was that all about Blakey", he asks.

I tell him my good news, and in his broad northern accent he says;

"About bloody time", before locking the door.

I jump around my room in disbelief. I am extremely excited, but have to calm myself down, experience has taught me that it's not over until I'm on the other side of these high walls. It's hard not to enjoy the prospect of knowing I'll be home with Jess very soon.

Saturday 29th May 2010

I am awake this morning at 6.50am, excited at the prospect of going home, I still can't believe the news. My door is unlocked at 8.30am for a cooked breakfast which I always decline. I am tempted to phone Jess, but she was working at the club last night and will have only just fallen to sleep, by the look of her the last time she visited she needs to work less and sleep more. My news, as good as it is, can wait until she's had her well-deserved sleep.

I can wait no longer than 11.00am, and my phone call to her wakes her up. She is over the moon with the news. We chat briefly before I let her go back to sleep.

It is raining today so I choose to confine myself to my room. I don't want to share the news of my release with any other inmate out of consideration. It's great to see someone leave this awful place, but it also highlights the length left of your own sentence, and a certain amount of jealousy sets in. I don't want anyone to be jealous of me so my lips stay tight, though the instant change in my mood may give it away.

3.30pm I phone Jess for the second time to find that the news has sunk in, and she is busily preparing for my return. She wants to know which day in the week she can drive away from HMP Stafford with me in the passenger seat. I haven't been given any more details as to when I walk through the gates to my new life, but I tell her it's likely to be Friday at the latest. I don't want to spend another weekend in here, even though I have the luxury of the facilities G Wing boasts.

4.30pm dinner and bang-up, not long to go now Ash.

Sunday 30th May 2010.

Nothing to report.

Monday 31st May 2010. Bank Holiday

The weather is half decent today allowing G Wing residents to enjoy the well-kept gardens. JT and I stroll around chatting until I happen to look up to notice faces in the window of my cell, sorry room. I am summoned up to find three officers, including Mr. Hancock, sat in my room. I am informed that it is a cell search and my name came out of the hat. I offer to make them tea while they carry out their search. Of course there is nothing untoward to be found in my room, so we sit chatting like old friends.

When I speak to Jess at 3.30pm she sounds happy having spent the night celebrating her best friend's birthday, enjoyed all the more knowing that I'll be home soon.

4.30pm bang-up another day over.

Tuesday 1st June 2010.

The day passes with the usual routine, I am hoping to be told which day I'll be going home, and ask Mr. Hancock to chase it for me. By the evening he has no news for me, and I go to bed with that familiar feeling of anticipation.

Wednesday 2nd June 2010.

Today marks my nine month anniversary of being banged up. Every second, minute, hour, day, week, month has taken an eternity to pass.

Off to the gym at 8.45am to put in a lacklustre performance, I just can't be bothered. Still no news comes my way until I phone Jess at 7.00pm. She's spoken to my probation officer, and has the latest for me. Governor Small now wants to attach conditions to my HDC License asking me not to take any other employment other than that which I have detailed in my letters to him, but this first needs to go before another board to decide whether this is actually allowed to happen. The news means more delay, plunging my ecstatic mood back to where it had been for much of the past nine months.

Thursday 3rd June 2010.

I decide to become the squeaky cog hoping to get the oil today, and ask Mr. Hancock to chase a release date for me before heading off to the gym.

The gym is hard work, not physically, but mentally draining. As much as I try to keep to myself, and away from the mindless banter and bull shit on constant drip from the mouths of inmates, the more they seek me out. Frustrated and pissed off at the prison's incompetence I just don't have the patience to deal with them this day.

Lunch time, like all time in prison, takes an age to arrive, when it does Mr. Hancock has news for me. He's been to the department that deals with the release of prisoners to fight my corner. He tells me that all the paperwork has been prepared, but is awaiting the signature of Governor Small. However, Governor Small is on holiday until next week. When he suggested to the clerk that the deputy Governor should sign it she sifted through my paperwork to find that Governor Small had already signed it off, two days ago. The clerk starts my release procedure and, off the record, Mr. Hancock tells me I'll be gone by Tuesday. This information should be fabulous news to my ears, however, if the person responsible for the release paperwork had done their job properly I'd have been going home tomorrow. I have been on an emotional rollercoaster for the last year or so, not least the last seven weeks. I decide I need to see it in writing before I can really believe I'm going home.

I phone Jess, she's also been given the news of my release from my probation officer which provides some sort of confirmation.

Friday 4th June 2010.

By lunch time the paperwork I've been so desperately awaiting has arrived. It confirms I am going home on Tuesday.

FORM HDC(5)   NOTIFICATION OF PROVISIONAL ACCEPTANCE FOR HOME
               DETENTION CURFEW

SECTION ONE: PRISONERS DETAILS

Surname: **Blake**	Forename(s): **Ashley**
NOMS Number: **A3043AH**	Date of Birth: **15/07/1969**
Prison Number: **CN7762**	

Proposed date of release on HDC: **08/06/2010**	Curfew hours:					
Proposed address of curfew:	Start	Mon	**19:15**	End	Mon	**07:15**
		Tue	**19:15**		Tue	**07:15**
27		Wed	**19:15**		Wed	**07:10**
Hadzor Road		Thu	**19:15**		Thu	**07:15**
Oldbury		Fri	**19:15**		Fri	**07:15**
West Midlands		Sat	**19:15**		Sat	**07:15**
B68 9LA		Sun	**19:15**		Sun	**07:15**
	Curfew hours on day of release: **15:00** until **07:15**					

You have provisionally been assessed as suitable for release on Home Detention Curfew, subject to the continued availability and suitability of the address given above. This decision may also be reversed should your subsequent behaviour or any new information demonstrate that you should no longer be considered suitable.

This information will be disclosed to the electronic monitoring company responsible for monitoring your whereabouts. They may contact others at the above address in advance of your release.

If for any reason the proposed curfew address given above becomes unavailable, you must immediately inform a member of staff. You may be asked details of to provide alternative address.

Once released on Home Detention Curfew you may be liable to be recalled to prison if <u>any</u> of the following happen:

(i)   You fail to remain at your curfew address during any part of your curfew hours, or otherwise fail to comply with your curfew conditions.
(ii)   The curfew address can no longer be electronically monitored.
(iii) It is decided that you pose a serious risk to public safety.
(iv)   You are charged with a further offence while on Home Detention Curfew.

If you are serving a sentence of one year or over, or you are a young offender you will also be subject to other licence conditions and will be supervised by the Probation Service. You will be given a licence to sign before you are released which will give details of the licence conditions which will apply to you.

Signed: _P. Moreland_   Name: _MORELAND_

Grade: _PSM F_   Date: _3/6/10_

The weekend before I am released is long
hot and boring. I get through it with
thoughts of this time next week, and plans

for my future with Jess. I still choose not to tell other inmates of my imminent departure, and carry on the usual routine.

Monday 7th June 2010. Day before release.

Attend the gym as usual. It isn't until leaving the gym for my last time that I am overheard saying goodbye and thanking the gym officers. It is too late for my gym buddies to play any practical jokes on me which is the traditional way of wishing someone farewell. The news soon travels along the line of inmates filing back to their respective wings. From the other side of the high mesh fence shouts of;

"Nice one Ash", all the best mate",
"See you on the outside",
"Don't come back" and so on.

It is only then that JT and Mark Botfield learn I am to go. Though very pleased for me Mark still has two years to serve, and he has to witness me leaving, that cannot be a good feeling.

This evening I am more popular with visits to my room than ever before, for two reasons: 1. People want to wish me well, and 2. People want my stuff.

I pack up my cell and give much of my stuff away, apart from one last night with my feathered pillows and duvet.

I phone Jess from the wing phone booth one last time, and tell her how much I am looking forward to leaving this place with her. I warn her that there may be photographers waiting outside so she is not to be late, and we can escape without having to go through the publicity which she's come to hate.

I am locked away at 7.45pm, lights out 10.30pm.

Tuesday 8th June 2010.

I wake to grey skies and drizzling rain outside my window, but in my dark cell all I can see is the bright lights of freedom beckoning. My door is unlocked at 7.50am, I am the only inmate unlocked. As I make my way down the corridor with my large box of mainly letters, my neighbours come to say goodbye and good luck through the crack in their doors. I usually hate goodbyes, but this one I really enjoy.

I shake the hands of Mr. Hancock and Mr. Major, thank them for looking after me, and leave G Wing. I am taken across to reception, given £36.00 release money, and two sports type bags to transfer whatever was in my box into. I sign various bits of paperwork and am led to the main entrance. One last confirmation of who I am to the gate officer then, with the press of her button, the large steel blue gates I entered through months ago begin to slide to the right, just enough to let me through. I step out into freedom, brace myself for the snappers, but more importantly to throw my arms around my Jess.

THE END

The Final Blow

Jess and I are still great friends and speak every week on the telephone. She wants no part of this book and has asked, pleaded on many occasions, for me to change her name. However, I've refused as I truly believe had it not been for her I would not be here today. Jess did meet someone through work at her friend's club as I feared all along, it was inevitable. Having said that, she has told me that she did not take the relationship further until I was out of jail.

In the months following my release we talked, cried and argued, and we tried desperately to make things work, but the pressure of the whole ordeal had taken its toll on Jess and she wanted none of it. She was angry at the way I'd been treated, and bitter with the law, something had to give. Sadly it was our relationship. We parted as great friends, and for that at least, I'm grateful.

Lightning Source UK Ltd.
Milton Keynes UK
UKOW021043081011

179887UK00003B/2/P